"Joan hit the mark!

As a leader, providing feedback to your team is one of the most valuable things you can do. Clarity on direction and expectations is a cornerstone for senior leaders. The ultimate goal is ensuring your team knows what's expected so they can execute against it. Over the past 35 years I have learned there are no straight lines.

Companies and people tend to tack left and right like sailboats as they move toward their goals—and the only way you can reach your destination is with honest, constructive and frequent feedback."

— David Mattson, CEO, Sandler

"We are all being impacted by rapid technological advances in the workplace and beyond, and perhaps the most important capability that will separate us from our machines is our ability to give timely, honest, caring, and constructive feedback. Joan's real-life stories peppered throughout the book inspire confidence for even a first-time leader. *The Leader's Guide to Mastering Feedback* is a must-read for every leader aspiring to create a thriving, high-performance team and foster a culture of growth and human flourishing."

— Brian Mohr, Co-Founder & CEO, anthym

"This book is a valuable guide and reference for those who want to learn the art of giving feedback. Joan, through her personal stories and deep wisdom, has created a roadmap for you to become masterful at giving feedback. You will get your voice heard gracefully—just as Joan does."

— Lynne Brown, Executive Coach/Consultant

"*The Leader's Guide to Mastering Feedback* is an extraordinary work that will undoubtedly leave a profound and lasting impression on leaders who dare to take their teams to new heights. It is an essential read for any leader who values excellence, growth, and the extraordinary power of feedback."

— Dan Perez, President & CEO, Subrosa Investigations

"Every leader at every level needs to read this book. Joan has built the bridge over the feedback chasm that we all suffer from and that only seems to grow wider through our discomfort when giving or receiving feedback. This very clear 'how-to' book will completely change your attitude around giving and receiving feedback. Masterfully done."

— Michael Norton, Executive Vice President, Sandler Enterprise Division

"I have been teaching leaders around the world the importance and impact of delivering critical feedback for years. I can attest to the immense impact of feedback on the growth and success of a team. This book is a game-changer, and I wholeheartedly recommend it to any leader who aspires to make a lasting difference in the people they work with. Joan has woven together a unique reading experience that is bolstered by research as well as experiences.

Critical feedback is so named because it references both critique and importance. Unfortunately, many leaders shy away from it because they don't know how to do it confidently. Joan has given the business world a much-needed tool to enhance the efficacy and confidence of delivering important feedback."

— Eric M. Bailey, Bestselling Author and
Organizational Psychology Professional

"What a gift! Joan's brilliance is certain to transform our workplaces and our world. Not only does she provide a relatable framework and tools for mastery of feedback, but the equally important context for why it matters and how it can reshape and enhance our human connections."

— Tracy Morrissey, HR Professional/Consultant

"One of the book's remarkable strengths lies in its emphasis on the positive impact of feedback when it is approached with empathy and respect. By encouraging leaders to build trust and cultivate a safe environment, it empowers them to engage in candid and open conversations with their team members. *The Leader's Guide to Mastering Feedback* offers actionable strategies to turn feedback sessions into opportunities for growth, ensuring that each interaction propels individuals and the organization forward."

— Susan Drumm, JD, MA, MCC, Bestselling Author of *The Leader's Playlist*

"When pockets of gossip and mistrust affected our team, it was hard to know what to do. After several years of engaging in the practice of feedback through Joan's training and coaching, we have developed a culture of openness and continual feedback that really makes a difference in how we collaborate and get work done. Our organization was lucky enough to receive lessons on feedback directly from Joan. And now, these critical lessons, for everyone from executives to emerging professionals, can be widely shared and implemented thanks to *The Leader's Guide to Mastering Feedback*."

— Kris Skavish, Co-CEO, Two Octobers

"Virtually every leader I work with believes they are better at feedback skills than they actually are. This book addresses this essential aspect of leadership efficacy, offering comprehensive insights and step-by-step techniques to master the art of delivering constructive feedback. This book caters to leaders at every level, helping them navigate the complexities of giving feedback effectively."

— Evan J. Roth, Master Certified Coach

"Joan taps into one of the primary secrets of engagement and retention... the ability to give heartfelt and artful feedback to your team. She does not mince words but lays out a simple approach based on many years of experience. An approach that will absolutely 'stick' because it simply makes sense!"

— Dr. Beverly Kaye, Thought Leader, Author, Keynote Speaker

"This book not only provides practical techniques for delivering feedback effectively, but it also offers insights into receiving feedback constructively. Joan's ability to address both sides of the feedback equation makes this a well-rounded and holistic guide that can truly transform workplace dynamics by uplifting and supporting each other."

— Tamara Player, CEO

"In a world where effective leadership and continuous improvement are paramount, *The Leader's Guide to Mastering Feedback* stands as a beacon of wisdom and practical guidance. This outstanding book, authored by Joan Hibdon, will be an indispensable resource for leaders focused on creating an organizational culture where people feel connected, are thriving, and achieving crucial organizational results."

— Allie Gehm, COO, Subrosa Investigations

"I can't count how many times in my long leadership career I've talked about feedback—the importance of giving feedback, getting feedback, and the difference it can make. *The Leader's Guide to Mastering Feedback* is the first comprehensive and useful guide on this topic that I have encountered. Joan's personal experience, artfully woven in with data and tools, makes a point that is truly effective. I was particularly moved by the analogy of our employees being on stage performing for us, just as Joan performs musically for an audience, and the energy and beauty that comes from audience engagement (feedback), resulting in an amazing performance.

I strongly recommend this book to leaders at all levels and ages. I plan to make this a staple for our organization's leaders and can easily envision using the specific Reflections/Practices at the end of each chapter as tools for our team's development. I look forward to the feedback and results that come from our team!"

— Connie Perez, Healthcare Leader

"Honest and open dialogue between employees often defines how corporate cultures shape and evolve. Joan has tapped into this critical component for success."

—Marc Willency, Executive

"If you are a leader looking to master the art of giving feedback while empowering your team to achieve their full potential, this is the book for you. Joan provides practical advice on how to effectively offer feedback that is genuine, tailored to the individual, and supports and inspires growth. Her skillful use of real-life stories and analogies paints a clear picture of the importance of giving feedback and how to give it. The concepts she shares are easy to understand and apply. Her writing style creates an easy flow from story to concept and then to application.

This is a realistic guide that encourages leaders to adopt a mindset of self-awareness, self-discovery, and personal improvement. At the end of each chapter, Joan includes key reflections, questions, and a self-affirming takeaway, creating an interactive experience that encourages both learning and application."

— Rachel Lutowsky, Executive and Leadership Coach

"Joan's experience in the corporate and coaching world makes her uniquely qualified in offering feedback. Her passion for helping people combined with her workplace know-how creates a useful guide that will transform the culture of your organization. Everyone who communicates, and let's face it, that's all of us, can benefit from learning these skills!"

— Rose Snyder, ACC, CPIC, Rose Snyder Coaching and Consulting

THE LEADER'S GUIDE TO
MASTERING FEEDBACK

THE LEADER'S GUIDE TO
MASTERING
FEEDBACK

Transform Relationships and Results
One Conversation at a Time

JOAN R. HIBDON, CPCC, PCC

Published by jdhInsights Press

To contact the author about speaking or ordering books in bulk, visit www.jdhinsights.com

ISBN (paperback): 979-8-9887193-0-4
ISBN (ebook): 979-8-9887193-1-1

Editor: Mary Reynolds Thompson
Copyeditor: David Aretha
Proofreader: Steve Scholl
Book design: Christy Day, Constellation Book Services
Publishing consultant: Martha Bullen, Bullen Publishing Services
Author photo: Teri Spillan

Library of Congress Control Number: 2023915435

Printed in the United States of America

For my dear friend Anne Rackerby.
A beautiful friend who delighted in life and who
taught me to be the woman I have become.

Treat feedback as a gift rather than a slap in the face.

~Frank Sonnenberg

Contents

How Feedback Changed my Life

Communication—the human connection—
is the key to personal and career success.

~Paul J. Meyer

Early in my working life, I set a goal to climb the corporate ladder. I went to university part-time while working full-time with the intention to learn, develop, and rise within the business system as quickly as possible. As a high achiever, I had my sights on a top-level position in my profession and industry of choice.

By my early forties, I was part of a leadership team with a tele-communications organization. My role was to manage a learning and development group of up to twenty-five people responsible for creating and delivering training development for all areas: sales, technology, product, process, systems, tools, and management/leadership training.

I enjoyed the challenge and hard work that went along with helping people grow and develop. I was doing what I loved: leading people, managing projects, collaborating with other leaders, and making key decisions. I liked getting things done. I was also trying to stand out in a sea of talent and prove myself more than capable of achieving the strategic expectations established by our leadership team. I oversaw my team juggle scores of critical projects at a time. Our work was critical to the organization's success and everyone on the team was committed to the task of transforming the very nature of how learning was being provided throughout the organization. My talented team thrived in the innovative environment.

I loved being part of the "A" team. Better yet, we all genuinely cared about one another. This was evidenced in how we connected, collaborated with, and trusted one another.

Of course, every job comes with its challenges. Like many organizations, then and now, we were continuously innovating and often had too many competing and shifting priorities. With all the changes, it was common to experience communication breakdowns. And, typically, we never had enough time or resources to do all the work, which proved frustrating at times.

The executive team knew the number of projects we were working on, but based on my experience, lacked awareness of how long it took to develop and deliver engaging learning content. This resulted in our receiving insufficient resources of time and support. And, on occasion, recognition of the value we were delivering.

It wasn't uncommon for my team to work on 70 different projects at once. To track all the projects, we used the best system available to us—a good old-fashioned Excel spreadsheet. It offered a detailed view of projects and created a visible way to instill confidence that my team was focused on delivering the right training projects, to the right teams, at the right time. There was a lot going on, and every time a request came in for a new training, we captured requirements, and, in most cases, my standard answer was "Yep, we've got it." The Excel spreadsheet, our go-to-roadmap, was always packed with details of each project and multiple impacts to the organization.

One afternoon, I met with an executive I'd come to know well over my six years with the organization. I had an easygoing and trusting relationship with Marc and was looking forward to reviewing the overall training roadmap and how it aligned with the organization's business goals and needs. There was a lot to cover during this meeting.

As I reviewed the upcoming training details with Marc, I wanted to be certain that he was confident my team would deliver what his team needed. About halfway through our scheduled meeting time, Marc sat back from the table, put his hands on the table, took a deep breath, and said, "Joni, you know I care about you, right?"

I responded quickly with, "Yes. I know." And even as I said it I felt an uneasiness in my gut. In truth, I wasn't quite sure what his initial statement meant, but I intuited it wasn't business as usual.

"Joni," Marc began, "you have to stop being so f___ing nice."

I looked at him in surprise and asked, "What are you talking about?"

Marc looked down for a moment before returning my gaze. "Listen. We all know you want to make sure our organizational requests and needs are taken care of. It's clear in the full array of training commitments you have mapped out here. We know that you want to please us and want us to be confident that your team can take care of the organization's overall training objectives. We also know that you cannot do everything we are asking you to do with the people and resources you have. Bottom line, by continuing to accept our requests you are putting your team, other projects, and the organization at risk."

I reeled from his comments, confused. Was the leadership team aware that we could not do everything we were being asked to do? And they requested it anyway? Did it mean I had the choice to say "No" to any of the requests? Why was I just realizing this now?

Was I putting the organization at risk? I let Marc's words sink in. Surely, I cared too much about the organization to put it at risk. Wasn't that why my team and I were working so hard (nights, weekends) to deliver?

My brain took a few moments to catch up with his words. And then I got it. My desire to belong to this amazing group of leaders *had influenced my need to please and to accommodate every request. These subconscious desires were getting in my way of seeing the full strategic picture. I was putting my team at risk. I was pushing them too hard. And, if I was honest, I could see that I was putting projects at risk too. As these realizations bubbled up, I wrestled with the realization that saying "no" was an option. I hadn't known that. In fact, my direct boss, when confronted with the challenges we faced, would summarily respond, "The work needs to be done. You need to figure it out." If I asked for more resources, he would say, "You should look at the resources you have. Are they right for your team?" [More on this later in the book.]*

Marc sat patiently while I thought everything through. And then we had the real conversation. I learned from Marc that everyone cared about me, and they wanted me and my team to be successful. However, they had noticed that as a leader, I tended to accommodate the requests of the other leaders without considering the impacts on my team, peers, and the organization.

We spent the remainder of that meeting talking more about what was needed and who I needed to be as a leader to deliver the critical projects and results, without agreeing to unrealistic demands.

As I left Marc's office, I made a quick detour to the restroom. Checking to ensure that no one else was there, I sobbed for several minutes. I had never in my life felt so "naked." On the one hand, I was mortified that Marc—and, I was guessing, others—were able to see how much I wanted to please. On the other hand, it felt like a huge weight was being lifted from my shoulders.

A few days later, I decided to confirm Marc's feedback with others, including my boss, certain executives, and my peers. Without hesitation, when I shared what Marc had said to me, everyone I spoke with concurred that they too had similar concerns.

It was clear my approach was off. I needed to work on myself to understand my compulsion to please, accommodate, and make everything better. I hired an executive coach and began to dig deep into what I came to call my *Pleasing Polly* tendencies, which stemmed from childhood. I asked my older siblings about when we were young. In one conversation, I remembered hiding in my sister's bedroom with my four siblings when things got heated between Dad and Mom. Until, that is, I could bear it no more and ran out of the room crying and begging my parents to stop fighting, saying, "I'll be good, I promise!" Then and there, I adopted the belief that if I was a "good girl," doing what I was asked and being agreeable, I'd make everything better. I could fix what needed to be fixed. No wonder *Pleasing Polly* was a part of me. Now it was time to make different choices.

I began to pay attention to when I was taking on responsibilities that were realistic and manageable, versus with the intention to please others. Was I agreeing with something because I "did agree" or did I just "want to please"? If the latter, I would stop the conversation and allow myself to "reframe" with the purpose of "breaking the unconscious habit of pleasing" I had developed over a lifetime.

I was learning a lot about myself. I was also now attuned to what I had been modeling for my co-workers and began to notice what needed correcting.

I checked in with my team more frequently. How were they doing? Were they over-extended, comfortably busy, or in need of more projects to work on? Based on those conversations, I was able to shift responsibilities between the training consultants. I also shared with my team what I was learning about myself and invited them to be transparent and curious with me about when I was taking on too much for myself or them.

Throughout, I was learning to pay attention to what I was saying "yes" to, "not now" to, and "no" to. My answers were now based on organizational priorities, my team's availability, and the tools and/or resources available. My behavioral shift made a substantial difference. For the remainder of my tenure at that organization, I silently thanked

Marc for his feedback. It was transformational, not just for me but for my team and the organization.

To this day, I call Marc every year close to the anniversary of that conversation to thank him for "changing my life." He always laughs and says, "Joni, it wasn't that big of a deal."

My response is, "It was to me. Your being open and willing to provide this feedback to me changed my life. Period. I wouldn't be where I am today if it weren't for you."

———————————

Feedback is one of the most powerful yet least utilized communication skills employed across organizations today. As a Leadership Coach and Organizational Consultant, much of the work I do with leaders and teams stems from challenges directly tied to the absence of direct and compassionate feedback. Lack of engagement, poor performance, and underwhelming results can all be symptoms of this deficiency.

I am committed to cultivating inspiring leadership so that employees have extraordinary experiences at work. Building a culture of feedback into an organization is one of the key outcomes of the work I do in organizations today.

I'd be lying if I said Marc was the first to offer me feedback on my leadership style. My direct manager and his boss both tried. The difference was that I felt "judged" by their superior tone and intimidating body language. Their words felt shaming, in a similar way to the "red font" that bled all over a draft of a report I once wrote. My direct manager even phrased his feedback to me this way: "My noble intention in telling you this is...." His words made me feel small, less than. And no wonder. The word *noble* confers the privilege of being of high social or political class or possessing high moral principles. Got it. He was telling me he was—and knew—better than me. I shut down. How we give feedback, it turns out, really matters.

I still carry an image of sitting across from my direct manager. He had one foot on his desk and was leaning back in an office chair, arms crossed in front of his body. His posture and superior smile were so uncomfortable, they prevented me from buying one word of his feedback. If you'd been in my seat, I don't believe you'd have taken his words to heart either. Unlike when Marc spoke to me, mutual respect, trust, and connection were glaringly absent. Looking back, I realize my managers weren't necessarily trying to "put me in my place" or "put me down." They were, in their own way, trying to help me out with their feedback. That said, over many years of studying feedback, I have learned that those who are uncomfortable with giving it tend to come off as intimidating and superior. Afraid of confronting or upsetting an employee, they feel they must take full control of the conversation and protect themselves from any emotional reactions that ensue.

Providing effective feedback is an "art." It takes the ability to balance openness, directness, and courage with compassion, curiosity, and the willingness to be vulnerable. While not impossible, this is a tall order. No wonder most of us aren't natural at giving feedback. But the beauty is, we all can learn how to get better at it. And if you're in a position of leadership—a manager, supervisor, team leader, solopreneur, influencer—then please know this book will be a work and life changer.

If people count on you to inspire and influence others to achieve better results, if you are interested in the growth and development of your peers and employees, this book will show you how to provide heartfelt, artful feedback that can uplift your team, reinvigorate your company mission, create engagement, and improve performance. By the end of this book, I promise you, having read the stories, participated in the exercises, reflections, and practices, you will have the ability to seamlessly weave productive feedback into your everyday work exchanges.

The results will speak for themselves. I've worked with CEOs and other C-Level leaders, heads of HR, people who are in executive level or middle manager positions, owners of small and large businesses, and people who are hired into working teams. Every single person has said that providing clear feedback is key to their success. What's more, they appreciate how learning to give feedback has also made them open to receiving it. And yet, feedback is what they struggle with the most. Why is that?

I believe when feedback is offered with compassion—when it is heartfelt and relational—it creates stronger connections between people. However, most don't offer feedback from that place of relationship. We can often sound harsh, dismissive, or judgmental. And feedback like that is miserable to give and even worse to receive. The result? We stay clear of it. And yet, whatever you feel about feedback, it's important to realize that it occurs all the time. That's right. A raised eyebrow, a smile, a certain tone in one's voice . . . we are always signaling what we think. These messages are easy to misread. They can cause all kinds of problems and confusion. So let me say this clearly: Feedback is important and it's here to stay. But bringing it out into the open is critical if you want to create healthy connections and thriving relationships.

There's magic to feedback. It is one of the most powerful professional tools at your disposal. And yet it is a skill most leaders I meet, and most people I work with, are poorly versed in. Then again, if you had the art of giving feedback mastered, you wouldn't be reading this book. But don't worry, even if you are presently uncomfortable with feedback, the stories, facts, reflections, and practices contained in these pages will help you develop your own style, confidence, and competence in mastering this important art. So, let's take a quick look at how you can move from being a Feedback Freshman to a full-on Feedback Master.

This book is divided into short chapters. Depending on where you are starting from, you can read this book chronologically or skip around depending on the core feedback element you'd like to learn and practice.

Chapter 1: What Is Feedback? Learn what feedback is in the corporate setting, the different types of feedback, and how feedback sets the course for your organization.

Chapter 2: The Benefits of Giving Feedback. Learn what can be achieved through feedback and structured strategies to help you to give feedback in a beneficial way.

Chapter 3: The Cost of Not Giving Feedback. Learn the risks to your bottom line, reputation, and relationships by not providing feedback.

Chapter 4: How Energy Is a Form of Feedback. Learn how to master your energy to create the best outcome when giving feedback. Whether or not you verbally give feedback, your energy speaks volumes.

Chapter 5: Creating the Optimal Environment for Feedback. Learn how feedback is hastily given and without consideration for external conditions can put that feedback at risk. Then discover how to select the optimal environment that will help ensure receptivity and connection between the feedback giver and receiver.

Chapter 6: A Unique Way of Thinking About Feedback. Learn how playing with different perspectives, or wearing different hats, can achieve creative solutions and leverage feedback even more effectively.

Chapter 7: Why Feedback Is Core to Leadership. Not only is feedback important in our working relationships and output, but also it is a skill that can instantly strengthen the integrity, power, and performance of someone in a leadership role. Leading with feedback, when understood well and executed with care, is one of the best things a leader can do.

Chapter 8: Things that Get in the Way of Giving Feedback. Learn about the anxieties, fears, stories, and taboos wrapped up in giving feedback. This chapter breaks down and points out a few of those common feelings/thoughts and helps you free yourself to be yourself.

Chapter 9: Ghosting: A Contemporary Twist on Feedback. Learn about the growing phenomenon of ghosting and how damaging it can be to organizations and employees.

Chapter 10: Being on the Receiving End of Feedback. Learn how to be as good at receiving feedback as you are becoming at providing it—and see how these two things are linked.

Chapter 11: Giving Yourself Permission to Offer Feedback. Imagine what the world would look like if we were all able to "dance with feedback," growing with each step.

As you map out your journey with this book, within each chapter you'll find an amusing or interesting fact to consider about feedback. At the end of each chapter, I've provided specific instructions for practice or reflection. These are intended to invite you to sit with each chapter and explore how the topic of feedback sits with you. While feedback is a universal communication skill, how we each interpret, perceive, and engage with this skill is unique to each one of us.

Final and Important Notes

This book and the practices are designed to create a masterclass of sorts, to help you become artful at feedback. Like with anything worth having, practice makes perfect. The more you engage in the practices and exercises, the more you will find this roadmap for providing feedback a perfect recipe for success. However, I can guarantee that even just reading through examples and practices about giving feedback will shift your relationship to feedback entirely. Whether you're someone who "dives in" or someone who doesn't, this book will make a difference in your life.

One final note: the many stories shared throughout these pages are based on actual people and events. To ensure anonymity, however, I have changed some of the names and circumstances.

My invitation to you right now is to take a moment to think about how you feel about feedback. Reflect on any feedback you've already provided today. What do you remember about your expression, your tone, your pace of language, and your words? What impact did your feedback have on the other person?

Now, let's begin. As you turn this page, we'll jump in and explore feedback with curiosity, courage, compassion, and authenticity. Let's see if we can create some great feedback moments for you.

CHAPTER 1

What Is Feedback?

And Why Does the Work Environment Call for It, Especially Today?

By creating a feedback culture within your office,
you ensure that people continue to learn, grow,
and challenge themselves.

~Neil Blumenthal

The results of a 360 report had been compiled, and I was going through it with my client, a VP of a large financial investment company. The report contained the answers to certain questions about the VP, given by her boss, peers, direct reports, and others. Hence the name 360.

My client had reviewed the report in advance of our debrief, allowing her the opportunity to privately digest the information. "What are your initial observations?" I asked. She responded, "You know, I'm grateful for this feedback. I've been asking for feedback off and on for the twelve years that I have been at this company and in my role. And you know, what? I've received the "You're doing a good job" kind of feedback. But nothing meaningful or actionable. What I hate, though, is that it's taken twelve years to receive comprehensive feedback I can do something with. I'm guessing that what I am seeing here is an indicator of my behaviors since the beginning of time. Imagine where I would be today if someone had exhibited the courage or the skill to provide me with this kind of feedback ten years ago. I would have already course corrected. As it stands today, I feel like a bit of a failure. As if people have been standing by and watching me flounder in these areas and that no one has said anything."

She went on to say, "It truly is lonely in top leadership positions. I'm guessing that my boss and peers don't know how to give feedback to me or others because I'm 'a VP and should know better.' And my direct reports certainly won't give feedback because, well, I'm 'a VP and the boss and should know better.' And you know what? I'm human. I too need to grow and develop to be the best leader I can be."

She ended by saying, "While it's uncomfortable to receive this feedback, I know that it's being provided at the right time and honestly, I'm ready for it."

I thought for a few minutes and then responded, "I want to acknowledge these insights you've shared. As you have reviewed this feedback, I admire how you have chosen to sit with this input and perhaps have felt discomfort with what you're absorbing. I appreciate and value your desire to grow through this experience. I also want to remind you that everything highlighted in your 360 report fits into the coaching goals we've already identified. Your initial goals and your team's feedback are in alignment. That's great news. So, let's get to work…"

Early in my career, I trained new managers on how to give feedback using a licensed corporate training program. The concepts they were taught had to do with giving "performance" feedback, the type of feedback necessary for the traditional "annual" review and/or a final termination warning. Feedback like this requires planning, documentation, and the involvement of HR. It feels heavy and so is often put off as a last resort. Limited to performance reviews, feedback continued to feel exhausting and awkward for these managers. The training did not motivate managers to provide feedback as a normal course of business, nor did it alleviate the discomfort of offering feedback. Which offers insight into why someone like my client had to wait twelve years before she experienced constructive feedback.

So, here's the thing. The only way to become comfortable with this crucial skill is to practice it early and often. And to provide it for more reasons than just "performance" feedback. While feedback training, corporately licensed or otherwise, can help, if practice and reinforcement aren't part of the continuation of learning, the training will fall by the wayside.

I teach people to become comfortable with the uncomfortable. In other words, how to normalize feedback. To make it part of the everyday workings of an organization. The truth is that people **want** feedback. And they **need** it to grow.

To master giving compassionate and constructive feedback, you must practice. If you want to succeed at golf, you go to the driving range and hit bucket after bucket of balls. If you want to learn how to play a musical instrument, you choose one that interests you and then practice, practice, and practice. If you want to be a writer, you put pen to paper or fingers to keyboard, over and over again. In his blockbuster book, *Outliers*, bestselling author Malcolm Gladwell made popular the principle that you need 10,000 hours of deliberate practice to become an expert in any field. So, I say to you: to be a great leader requires patience, practice, and the willingness to sometimes fail. You will find yourself out of your comfort zone at times. But this too: In the end, it will be so worth it!

What Exactly Is Feedback?

Imagine you are on a sailboat in the middle of an ocean destined for a beautiful tropical island. The sails are hoisted, the lines are taut, supplies have been provisioned, and everything is in order. While sailing, you are distracted by the beauty of the water and the salty breeze. The gentle rocking of the boat on the waves has lulled you to sleep, and you fail to notice the wind has shifted and you have veered off course. When you awaken and check your waypoints, you realize you are no longer heading toward your beautiful tropical island. In fact, you're headed for dangerous and rocky waters. To get out of harm's way, you must quickly readjust the sails and man the helm, checking the waypoints every several minutes to ensure that you stay on the right course.

Feedback, then, is course correction. It is what allows us to reflect on whether we are still pointed in the right direction or whether we need to change something. It's about checking in and offering ways to help stay the course, meet our goals, keep a vision in our line of sight. The truth is, it's much easier to remain vigilant and make small tacks than to suddenly wake up and find yourself headed for disaster. So small course corrections, over time, add up to big benefits. Equally, neglecting feedback over time can have the opposite effect.

One of my first jobs was in human resources working for a growing national organization known for its awesome culture. Employees felt appreciated and valued, in part due to a carefully designed reward program that recognized contributions. Giving and receiving feedback was also integral to the culture. The organization took to heart employees' suggestions, implementing the ones that benefited the organization, and even provided feedback on the ones they didn't believe would work. Bottom line: the organization understood employees were their most valuable asset, and it showed.

I'd been with the company for four years when a new president was hired. Almost immediately the focus shifted. The new president placed metrics and profitability ahead of employees' well-being and inclusion. The impact rippled across the organization as employee morale plummeted and customer service declined. Employees made mistakes never experienced before. They also began to bad-mouth the company, expending both time and energy in being upset. I felt unsettled about what was happening and as a respected leader in human resources, I felt uncomfortable taking part in it. On one level, I understood the new president's strategy and even agreed that we needed more emphasis on metrics and profitable practices. It was the abrupt and seemingly uncaring way the shift was made that didn't sit well with me. We were out of balance. I tried several times to voice my observations, to provide feedback that these changes were pushed on the employee population too soon, too fast. My opinions were dismissed. I finally gave notice after receiving an offer for a new job.

I was surprised when I got a call from the president asking me to stop by his office. He wanted to know why I had chosen to resign from my position. I told him in so many words, "My role is to take care of one of the company's most valuable assets: the people it employs. I take that role very seriously. Given the recent change in leadership, the new organizational focus, and how changes are being implemented, I don't think the leadership team is demonstrating that care." I agreed with him that we needed to implement metrics and measurements of success. However, I made it clear that things had become quickly unbalanced and I wanted to work for a company that could balance profitability with valuing its employees.

The president looked at me thoughtfully and thanked me for my courage and for my feedback.

A few days later I was asked to meet with my boss, the head of HR.

When I arrived in her office, the president was sitting across from my boss. They asked me to sit down. The president thanked me again for my feedback and told me he had been thinking about what I'd said. He asked if I would consider staying on with the organization to help navigate the implementation of organizational changes in a different way than what we had been doing. He said that finding balance was important and had taken to heart the need to value employees, along with the bottom line. I chose to stay and remained with the company for two more years.

It's worth lingering here to break things down and consider the important sources of feedback in this story.

1. When the leadership and organizational changes were made abruptly, performance dropped (nonverbal feedback), evident in behavior, outcomes, and morale.

2. When employees' opinions (verbal feedback) were shared and ignored, valuable employees resigned (nonverbal feedback).

3. When the audience (i.e., the president) was ready to receive verbal feedback, he was able to hear and respond to it.

4. When feedback was considered, valuable employees were acknowledged, retained, and rewarded (verbal and nonverbal feedback).

5. Lines of communication were restructured for more "give and take" of key feedback to help navigate the necessary organizational changes to create balance across the culture, which improved organizational results and employee engagement.

You see, multiple sources of feedback were in play at the same time. While the president's business expectations and intentions were the right ones for the organization, the manner in which changes were implemented so drastically impacted the organizational culture that it affected customer service. It got back on course, only because the new president was able to learn from feedback.

You can see where I'm going with this: feedback matters. It matters a great deal.

Organizations suffer when they don't regularly take stock of how they're doing. The winds of change are everywhere in the business world, and it's easy to be blown off course without even realizing it. Which is why it is vital to constantly check in and provide feedback. *How are we doing? Are we still on course to meet [name the goal]? Have I checked in with my team yet? Have I spoken to that key employee who keeps dropping the ball?*

The sailboat is a handy metaphor for the way feedback works. In actuality most companies operate more like large cargo or container ships that must run smoothly while supporting multiple heavy containers (think business departments). And unlike a small sailboat, if a cargo ship shifts even slightly off course, it takes a great deal of time and effort to turn it around. The larger the organization, the more important it is to incorporate constant feedback based on external and internal conditions. This way, you can make frequent adjustments, keeping the entire organization aligned with the mission, culture, and goals. In doing so, you can be at the helm of the company determining the differentiator between success or a shipwreck.

As a leader, asking for and responding to employee feedback is essential to retaining talent. Organizations that want to keep skilled, loyal workers need to know how to constructively receive feedback. If the company is not looking for answers and is resistant to implementing change, asking for feedback can potentially turn more destructive.

I once worked for an emerging technology start-up in which a venture capital group had heavily invested. The goal of the VC was to make the company not only competitive but a leader in the industry. The CEO was approachable, warm, and relationship-oriented, He knew how to motivate others and inspired loyalty. His blind spot was a seeming lack of urgency and drive for results, which was challenging for the venture capital firm. The new investors expected faster results and brought in a CFO and CTO from Silicon Valley, both of whom were ambitious, matter-of-fact, prickly, and extremely results-oriented. They were there to disrupt and create urgency to obtain the necessary results and get the venture capital group the highest return on their investment—and fast.

Initially, the emphasis on results orientation was a great thing—the company needed to increase profitability. However, as the drive for results trumped the importance of relationships, a significant imbalance was created. People suddenly felt like "tools." They felt unseen, undervalued, and, on occasion, bullied. Different from the CEO, the new CFO and CTO were difficult to warm up to. If these three key leaders could have leveraged their strengths as individuals by balancing relationships with results, an amazing outcome and culture could have emerged. Instead, the organization experienced an overnight increase in annualized turnover at an all-time high of 34 percent.

As the head of HR, I recommended we hire an external consulting firm to launch an anonymous employee engagement survey to gain insights on what was causing disengagement and departure from the organization. The leadership team tentatively agreed. After several months of interviewing reputable engagement survey companies, an independent consulting company was selected to handle the process. To ensure we had buy-in, the executive leadership team provided input on the questions being asked. This created a sense of influence and control of the outcome.

When we launched the survey, the consulting firm said it was common to get a 30-40 percent response rate, and only if employees trusted that their responses would remain anonymous. We received a 53 percent response rate. When the results came back, the feedback from the employees overwhelmingly indicated that the leadership team was the problem. The mandates, the directives, and, most importantly, the negative way they were being treated by this new group of leaders were the drivers of discontent. This feedback was a critical turning point for the organization. The leadership team was upset, choosing to believe the feedback came from a bunch of "troublemakers." They disregarded the report, blaming instead the employees, the consulting firm, and even me for bringing all this information to the surface.

It was the worst-case scenario. Beyond anything I could have ever imagined. Initially, I believed that the group of leaders I worked with would be interested in looking at the organizational challenges and be open and responsive to what they'd learned. I was wrong. As I look in the rearview mirror, I recognize that the leaders were not prepared for the feedback, to look at themselves, to dig deep, and make the changes necessary to sustain and retain an engaged and committed workforce. And so, employees continued to leave. A situation that could have afforded a shift in direction was now nothing less than a shipwreck.

I was disappointed in the team that I was a part of for their lack of concern for the employee experience. It was brutally apparent that this organization of leaders wasn't ready to make the adjustments to create the kind of environment that employees could thrive in. And they weren't going to attempt to change course. I added my resignation to the list.

How could this disaster have been avoided? What would it have taken for the feedback to be received and acted upon? And how might it have turned out? I would like to think that if the leadership team had been curious about their own impact on people and not just the technical and financial results, they might have responded in an open and self-observant manner. Who knows? I might still be working for them! Upon reflection, what I do know is that the leaders were expected to drive certain results for the organization at all costs, and in the end, it did cost them. Experienced and skillful employees left in droves. Without the stable platform of employees committed to the company vision, the product solution, or the customer experience, it ended up costing them market share in the industry space. Today, this organization is not the market leader it always dreamed of being.

Feedback is a compass that enables companies to navigate the choppy waters of today's corporate environment. The way I see it, the business climate is going to remain in a state of complex flux. The impact of external market challenges, coupled with volatile social issues, political tensions, shifting work environments, and ever-increasing technological disruptions will exacerbate the desire for employees to feel a sense of safety and belonging at work. And that means employees will demand transparent, authentic, and inspiring leadership in the years to come. Feedback is the key communication skill and mechanism that keeps everything and everyone on course.

Strong leadership is critical to any organization. Leaders are responsible not only for their own performance, results, and development; they are also responsible for the success and growth of their employees. Whether a leader has one or 250 employees, the leader plays a key part in guiding employees to gain mastery in their roles. And in doing so, it helps to elevate the waters for all. What's more, as this book will show, constructive feedback is one of the most overlooked skills in creating dynamic, relational, and successful companies. Feedback, well, quite frankly, it rocks!

The History of the Feedback Loop

Feedback was first described in 1915 by Charles Proteus Steinmetz in the *Journal of the Franklin Institute*. It illustrates the point when a cable becomes grounded and the current at its end reverses, flowing back into the cable. Hence, a feedback loop. During this period, the use of the word was associated with the early forms of electronics: an electronic cable with a loop that takes output and feeds it back as input.

Most of us have experienced the effects of an electrical feedback loop. Think of a sound system, complete with microphones, speakers, monitors, and electric cables that plug into the instruments. If everything isn't balanced just right, you'll find the levels are off, and the sound experience is jarring for musicians and audience alike. It might even result in a terrifying and obnoxious screeching sound—one that alerts the sound engineer to make immediate adjustments. Feedback is a continual loop of information. Outputs and inputs, adjustments, and fine-tuning. While I am not an electrician, I can conclude that in relation to electronics and humans, feedback at its best grounds us. Feedback at its worst makes us recoil.

It wasn't until the 1950s that feedback was used in conjunction with psychological and human science theory. The first known association was made by Norman Wiener, philosopher and mathematician, who in his book *The Human Use of Human Beings* recognized feedback loops not only as being mechanistic or electronic, but as having an impact on human communications. He believed that the quality of a message (information), sent and responded to (feedback), was at the core of functionality, whether of a machine, organism, or human. In other words, the integrity of the feedback loop was as important to functional human societies as it was to mechanical systems.

As a musician, I've always had a particular awareness of feedback, and not just regarding sound equipment. On the less technical side, there is an unspoken yet real and agreed upon relationship between the performer and the audience. The person on stage is there to enlighten or entertain. Most experienced performers can sense the mood in the room, and whether they are hitting all the right notes— metaphorically and otherwise. I remember performing an original song in Grand Lake, Colorado that I had played hundreds of times before. The audience danced, swayed, and clapped to the beat, clearly into it. I had never had an audience respond to that song with such visible enthusiasm. The energy was palpable and uplifting, and I found my energy matching theirs as I engaged and connected with them at a whole new level. Their feedback was feeding me, lifting me up, and taking me places I never could have imagined.

Conversely, I've had situations where my performance fell flat. It wasn't the right song for that audience, or I was just not "on." Whatever the reason, I felt a lack of response. When you are tuned into the energy of a room you can sense when something is off. My bet is that you've had similar experiences. Those in which your ideas or a talk have been met with enthusiasm, and you've felt unstoppable. And others where you've noticed that people aren't engaged. Performers or not, we are all being rated, all the time, whether we ask for feedback or not. And nothing is worse than being given the cold shoulder and not knowing why. I always try and get an honest answer from a friend in the audience as to what they noticed about my performance, well-received or not. I want to get better. And I don't want to suck anymore than I have to! I imagine we all can agree on that.

What I want to say here is don't be afraid to receive feedback or to give it. But let's all be mindful that it really matters how we offer feedback. We don't want to be like the heckler I met one night who shouted obscenities at me. Which, as you can probably imagine, did nothing to make me more of a musician.

So, let's look at how we can learn and grow from feedback, by looking at the feedback loop.

The Feedback Loop Explained

Every time a musician, keynote speaker, actor, activist, author, thought leader, athlete, team manager, or employee steps on stage, a court, a field, or the workplace, feedback will follow. The feedback signals how well things are being presented, performed, communicated, or perceived. To make your mark, you must be willing to give, receive, reflect on, and adjust to feedback.

Let's see what a feedback loop looks like in this context.

Action: Someone performs a task, makes a presentation, delivers on a project, or performs on stage. That's the first step.

Feedback: Once the action occurs, feedback is provided.

Adjust: Next, the recipient of the feedback chooses to adjust (or not) the behavior or performance based on the new information they've received.

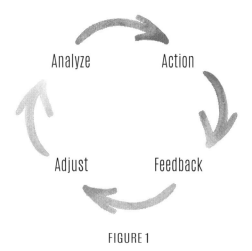

Analyze   Action

Adjust   Feedback

FIGURE 1

Analyze: The results of the shift in behavior are analyzed. Did it work? Was there an improvement?

And you are back to Action again.

This is a loop or cycle of events that is repeated over and over.

Let's consider for a moment my experience performing as a musician and walk through this loop.

I'm up on stage. I have my complete song list and I choose to perform a series of songs in front of an audience. The audience resonates with the music, their energy—clapping, dancing, and singing along. They provide me with feedback that I'm on the right track and I am encouraged to continue down that path. At the end of the show, I take stock of what worked for that audience (location, time of day, demographics, choice of songs, my own state of preparation, etc.). I note the information with the desire to create a similar experience next time I perform.

If the audience doesn't resonate with the music, I am at a crossroads with the feedback. I either choose to adjust and align with the energy of the audience, in which case I will likely end up in a space of resonance as I expressed above. Or, if I don't adjust, I will continue to feel the disappointment of being disconnected from the audience, who will remain disengaged and distracted. Without any adjustment, I can expect the same results as illustrated in Figure 2.

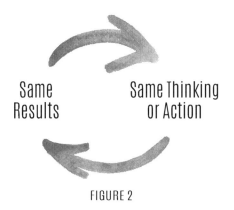

FIGURE 2

Taking this back into the workplace, consider this. Your employees are on a metaphorical stage performing for you. They want to know when you are standing in the stands, clapping for them and their success. They also need to know when you are not pleased with their performance. It may not always be easy for your employees to hear and accept your feedback. But if you remain silent, your team won't know what is required to adjust and grow.

As you begin to see the value in providing feedback, you may be wondering *how* to provide this feedback. Let me say upfront, there is no one-size-fits-all method, but rather a feedback "range." This range involves tone, among other things. At one end is the incredibly direct/caustic (think of a slap) approach and at the other, the "soft shoe" approach. Overall, it's important to stay somewhere in the middle and to learn how your employees prefer to receive feedback. Do you know how your employees like to receive feedback? If yes, congratulations! You fall into the small percentage of leaders or people who have dialed into this with your employees. If no, ask them.

Questions like, "How do you like to receive feedback?" "Do you want me to be direct?" "Do you need a moment?" "Do you want the good news or the bad news first?" Your employees, after all, are walking operating instruction manuals on themselves and how they can best take in your feedback.

There is also a feedback range that refers to the different methods of feedback. Let me provide you with a few examples:

- **Acknowledgment.** This is useful when recognizing someone's contribution, as in, "Thank you for your thought leadership on the project we've been working on together." Or "I appreciate you for the extra hours you put into our project. Your attention to detail has made all the difference." Statements like these ensure that people feel seen and that their hard work is recognized.

- **Praise.** "You were outstanding in onboarding our new employee. You made them feel 'at home' and helped them get up to speed on how we do things here." Praise is a notch up from acknowledgment, in that it moves beyond simply recognizing a contribution, by signaling that a person is a valued and indispensable member of the team and the organization. Praise is due to those who go above and beyond. What's more, it acts as an accelerant. Receiving praise feels so good, it encourages peak performance.

- **Curiosity.** "How did we get to this point in the project without researching the facts?" A question like this implies the problem, while avoiding personal attacks or criticism. It is a way of getting to the root of an issue without putting an employee on the defensive, and therefore keeps a line open for honest communication regarding the situation. "How do you think you did with that presentation? What did you do well and what could you do better next time?" Being curious, asking questions, allows a person to explore and examine their own performance while you, as the leader, either agree with their thinking or help them see where the problem may really reside.

- **Course correction.** "The report you produced had several errors and did not meet my expectations. Do you need more time to prepare?" Depending on the answer, you might ask, "What will ensure an accurate report next time?" What's important about this is that you are both setting expectations, inviting feedback, and being curious. Ideally this method creates a safe space for open conversation and connection, and the ability to course correct, so that you can get back on track.

- **Transparency.** This is where you just name what you see: "You weren't prepared." But don't stop there; your next move is an invitation to find the source of the problem, as in, "What happened?" Following the simple statement of fact with an open question creates a space for awareness and reflection without judgment.

There isn't a perfect or prescriptive way to provide feedback. There are different skills to practice and different ways to go about it. The more you practice, however, the more you'll find your own style, which is critical to your success as a leader. While I'll make lots of recommendations and offer lots of examples, you'll make your own decisions about giving and receiving feedback that serve your growth as a leader and your company's goals.

THOUGHTS ON FEEDBACK

Feedback is not bad or good; it depends on how it's delivered.

No one is perfect. We all have areas of growth, and feedback is a tool that helps us learn and get better. That's what most people want: to improve. No one ever wakes up and says, "I want to be bad at everything I do."

REFLECTIONS / PRACTICES

During a "quick" check-in with an employee at a client site, I asked about her experience of the job and the company. She replied, "This is the first professional job I've ever had. I've learned that feedback is important to me. I've been here for five months, and my boss hasn't given me any feedback on my performance."

If you're a boss in a company, it matters how often you provide feedback to your employees. And what I hear from employees is that they want feedback. I invite you to silence any voice inside saying, "I'll lose workers by giving feedback." Instead, tell yourself, "I'll retain more employees if I take the time to give them constructive feedback."

Now that you've read this chapter on What Is Feedback?, I encourage you to think about and write down some notes about:

- What does feedback mean to you?
- Why is feedback important to you?
- What is the most constructive feedback you've ever received? Why was it so helpful?

- What is the least effective feedback you've ever received? Why was it the worst?
- When you give feedback to someone, how do you want to be perceived or your feedback remembered?
- Are you giving enough and the right feedback to others? How do you know?
- When was the last time you gave feedback? How did it go?

Once you've completed this reflection, is there someone that you'd like to practice giving feedback to?

KEY TAKEAWAY

Learning and perfecting the art of giving feedback will make me a better leader and will transform relationships and results, helping my team become the best that they can be.

CHAPTER 2

The Benefits of Giving Feedback

We all need people who will give us feedback.
That's how we improve.

~Bill Gates

If you are going to take the time and effort to become an expert at giving feedback, then it's important that you first understand that feedback is a gift. In fact, it offers multiple benefits, including the four essential benefits I am about to expand upon. These benefits reflect ones my clients talk about when they start to experience the payoff of offering feedback.

Increased Results and Greater Connection

In September 2020, I met with a client of an organization focused on feedback and accountability. One of her requests to me was to check in with her individual team members regarding how the peer-to-peer feedback sessions were going. They were expanding their commitment about feedback, or as they called it, Exploring Criticism. I was excited to start working on this request, and, right away, we created agreements on deliverables and established due dates for my review.

Over the next several weeks, I scheduled individual meetings with each team member and compiled all the findings from each meeting into a list. Keep in mind, while I was doing this work, I was also working on several other projects for this client and juggling other clients' projects and needs.

Almost two months after the initial meeting, I received the following email message from my client: ". . . I wanted to check on your progress. When do you expect to have your summaries of the peer feedback interview completed, as well as tabulations regarding concerns? This task has been ongoing for a while. When we met for coffee, I talked about wanting to have you to help us make faster progress on identifying and addressing accountability, and I don't think we're really achieving that. I would like to get your thoughts based on what you know now so we can decide who/how to take this forward."

Oh boy. There it was. The feedback I had a sense would come and that I deserved due to the delay in my producing results. When I read her words, and in the context of our relationship, I perceived that I had let her down. All at once, I felt a jumble of emotions:

- *Shame.*
- *Disappointment in myself that I let her down.*
- *Grateful that she provided me with this feedback.*
- *A nano-second of defensiveness. Didn't she know that I had a lot of things I was working on for her? (I chose to let this one go like a "hot potato." Even I knew for myself that this was a BS excuse.)*

After a day of agonizing, I sent a text asking if my client could talk. This wasn't an email response kind of thing—her words warranted a conversation. I knew that to make things right, I needed to "clean up" the mess I had made and take ownership.

Upon connecting, the first thing I said was: "Thank you for having the courage to send me your feedback. Second, I want to apologize.

When I read your email, I felt such shame and sadness that I let you down. Our relationship means so much to me and I want to get this fixed. I'm also happy that you've mastered what we've been practicing and what we've been working on together: giving honest feedback. So where do we go from here?" We dove into a conversation that should have happened at least a month earlier.

As a result of my client providing this beneficial feedback, our relationship evolved and deepened. She gave me direct performance feedback and helped us both get clear on her expectations. Her feedback also caused me to think about professional areas I needed to develop so that I could better support not just her organization, but all my clients. And, finally, through this experience, the client and I are now capable of resolving conflicts quickly, intentionally, and effortlessly. The client relationship has ultimately grown both professionally and personally. And the organization is benefiting from the practice of feedback too.

#1 BOTTOM LINE BENEFIT:
INCREASED RESULTS AND GREATER CONNECTION

Giving feedback in a caring, curious, clear, and kind way is a gift. When you provide feedback from that place, it allows others to examine the situation and themselves. It also allows for the opportunity to collaborate in a more effective manner.

Course Correction

A small, emerging business was losing employees. The new CEO believed it was due to the company culture and hired me to assess what was going on. I was given the opportunity to speak with all employees. After completing my interviews, I presented my findings to the CEO and her team. A key theme emerged from the interviews: The way people spoke with one another and reacted to certain situations often made employees uncomfortable. I had understood respect to be a core value of the organization, but my findings said differently. In fact, it was reported that f-bombs or other swear words were flung about daily, which astonished me. Not only was the verbal communication reportedly unprofessional, but also the energy in the organization felt heavy, as if each employee was carrying extra weight on their back.

I shared my observations and findings with the CEO and her direct reports, many of whom used foul language. In fact, it had become so commonplace among the leadership team, they didn't even realize they were speaking this way. Once they received the feedback, however, they committed to cleaning up their language and to request a more professional tone across the workplace. They also committed to having me spend more time coaching leaders, engaging with employees, and facilitating team building.

This feedback and associated action made an immediate difference to the internal and external culture. The energy across the company felt less stressful almost overnight. While using swear words might not seem like the worst thing (we are, after all, each guilty of this at times), a culture of verbal disrespect is demoralizing. At worst, it puts everyone on edge. Facilitating employee meetings on how to create a culture, utilizing the core value of respect as the centerpiece, began the organization's transformation and put it back on course.

#2 BOTTOM LINE BENEFIT:
COURSE CORRECTION

Having the courage to provide feedback with the purpose of helping others see what they can't (blind spots) and experiencing immediate course correction is a tremendous benefit to people and organizations.

Improved Performance

A new salesperson, four months into the job, was underperforming in his role. My client, Zeb's manager, called to see if I could help his employee make progress. I began by speaking with the manager to gain an understanding of the performance issue. I then dove into reviewing the weekly and monthly sales results for the whole team, including Zeb. I also looked at the new employee onboarding expectations and training information. I was immediately able to see where the gap was between expectations and delivery. However, when I first sat down with Zeb, I wasn't sure what was causing him to underperform. I let him know that our meeting was at the request of his manager, and that I was there to coach on his job performance. I asked if he was open to working with me and he said, "Yes. I know I'm floundering and I'm not making my weekly or monthly sales goals."

I asked, "What's going on?"

"I don't really know. I'm still new to sales. Selling is harder than I thought and I'm trying not to get discouraged. I want to meet expectations, and I'm just not sure how."

"I think I know what's happening. Can I share with you what I see in your performance metrics?"

Zeb and I viewed his daily, weekly, and monthly reports together and I pointed to the problem. "Zeb, your daily outbound call expectation is fifty. On average, you're achieving forty-two calls per day. I think that's the missing link. If you're leaving eight calls (on average) on the table every day, that's forty calls per week. Imagine what you could achieve if you closed that gap."

Zeb's eyes widened. "I knew I was short on calls most days, but I didn't see the overall impact each week. What do I do?"

I spent more time with Zeb digging deeper into how he was operating on the outboard calls. After exploring his work tactics, I gave Zeb clear, direct feedback on immediate steps he could take to achieve his performance goals. I committed to checking in with him each week to ensure incremental and sustainable progress was being made. By the end of that first meeting, Zeb was energized, had a plan, and gained a new outlook on how he would accomplish the expected outbound calls each day. As agreed, I checked in with Zeb each week, and he exhibited continual improvement. Within thirty days, Zeb was comfortably meeting expectations.

#3 BOTTOM LINE BENEFIT:
IMPROVED PERFORMANCE

As a leader, it is your responsibility to pay attention to your employee's performance. When expectations aren't being met, you could partner with your employee (with or without the help of outside consultants) to curiously unpack why performance is impacted. From here, you need to provide the employee with specific performance feedback, and if offered with intention, both parties will generally achieve the desired outcome.

Creating Better Work Relationships

Casey came to our coaching call upset and blurted out, "I hate working with one of my co-workers. It seems like every time I'm in a meeting with this person and giving a report, he interrupts me. That alone is bad enough, but then he tends to repeat himself three or four different times on what I could be doing better, and he's not even in my department. This happens consistently and I'm sick of it! It's infuriating. It derails the entire meeting. Not only do we not resolve anything, but his interruptions also consistently extend the meeting past the scheduled time. I don't have time for this."

I asked Casey if she had provided any feedback to this co-worker.

Casey scoffed. "Absolutely not. The truth is, I don't think he would listen, and I wouldn't want to upset or have a conflict with him."

I asked, "So what is it that you have now?"

Casey paused and thought. "Hmm. I'm upset and creating an internal conflict with myself."

I asked, "How's that working for you?"

She smiled and said, "Well, you know . . ." After a few thoughtful minutes passed, Casey sighed. "You're right, I have to say something. Let's get to it. What coaching do you have for me?"

Casey decided she was interested in creating a better relationship with this peer and eliminating her internal conflict about the situation. She left our meeting with a new resolve to speak with her co-worker and provide him with feedback about how he was coming across in meetings.

Casey did speak with her co-worker and provided him with feedback. She let him know how his interruptions impacted her. As well, that his tendency to interrupt and to repeat things caused meetings to run longer than necessary. Her co-worker was surprised that she was so infuriated with him—he was only trying to help her with suggestions on how she could be more efficient. He also didn't know he repeated himself so many times. It wasn't a comfortable conversation. But as they talked through the issues they agreed that Casey would be more open to feedback and the co-worker would do his best to refrain from repeating himself.

#4 BOTTOM LINE BENEFIT:
CREATING BETTER WORK RELATIONSHIPS

Honing your ability to give and receive feedback reduces anxiety, animosity, and resentment, leading to greater connection and improved communication.

We've just reviewed four essential benefits of providing feedback:

- Increased Results and Greater Connection
- Course Correction
- Improved Performance
- Creating Better Work Relationships

Each of these benefits contributes to the creation of a strong culture that embraces feedback.

Now that you know some of the key benefits of providing feedback, let's explore some feedback practices that can be integrated into organizational culture. The regular implementation of these methods can help employees and organizations reduce the anxiety that often accompanies giving one-off feedback. Some of these systems in organizations include:

- **30-60-90 Day Interviews: Starting on the Right Foot**—The first ninety days is a critical period for a new employee and their manager. It helps the employee reflect on and share their experience of onboarding in their job with your company.

Monthly check-ins during this time provide an opportunity for the employee to meet with their manager or human resources representative and talk through a fixed set of questions.These meetings create value by ensuring employees have an opportunity to provide feedback on their initial experience in their job. It also creates the opportunity to learn about what's going well for the employee and, as needed, to address any initial concerns. This way, the manager and the employee can address any performance and/or job fit issues within the first 90 days and make necessary adjustments. Additionally, it sets the tone for the culture of feedback. The types of questions typically asked in these 30-60-90 Day Interviews can be found under Additional Feedback Tools.

- **Manager and Employee 1:1 Meetings (also called "Check-Ins" or "Touchbase")**—These meetings create the structure for a natural open feedback loop for a manager and employee. As a best practice these meetings are held weekly for a minimum of thirty minutes. The purpose of these meetings is for the manager to check in with an employee to see how things are going and to create a natural flow for open communication. As a manager, you may have several direct reports, a full meeting schedule, and a full in-box. If this is you, using your 1:1 meeting to establish communication practices with your employees will be helpful. For example, if you are super busy, you could ask your employee to hold all their questions for your regularly scheduled 1:1 so that your employees aren't adding to the chaos of your inbox. The types of questions typically asked in one-on-one meetings can be found under Additional Feedback Tools.

- **Skip Level Meetings**—These provide an opportunity for the manager's manager to connect with an employee with the purpose of asking for feedback about the employee's experience of their direct manager. This allows both parties to exchange information that contributes to the success of the employee and the manager. As a best practice, these meetings are held semi-annually and scheduled for an hour. Typical questions asked during this meeting can be found under Additional Feedback Tools.

- **2x2 Meetings**—These are helpful for providing feedback in bite-sized ways, and the structure of the meetings makes them very simple and straightforward. When two people meet to practice this meeting type, each person shares two things that the other person is doing well and two things that the other could do better. I recommend this be done in a very structured manner to reduce feelings of anxiety surrounding receiving constructive feedback. One person (Person A) should begin, saying to the other person (Person B), "The two things you are doing well are ____, and the two things you could do better are ____." After Person B receives this feedback, Person B says, "Thank you. I'll take that into consideration" or could ask clarifying questions specific to the feedback Person A shared. Then, Person B takes a turn following the same structure, allowing Person A space to ask specific questions after the feedback has been provided. Typical questions asked during this meeting can be found under Additional Feedback Tools.

- **Exit Interviews**—This final meeting in an employee lifecycle allows for closure when an employee leaves an organization. The employee provides feedback and insights for the company's consideration, which may help improve processes, procedures, and experiences. It also provides the opportunity for managers to receive direct feedback from their departing employees. In some cases, it is an opportunity for the company to provide feedback to employees too. Typical questions asked during this meeting can be found under Additional Feedback Tools.

Structured methods of feedback can benefit your organization as well as your personal life because they supply frameworks and practices to help you gain confidence and ease with giving and receiving feedback.

THOUGHTS ON FEEDBACK

Offering Feedback Provides Input that Breeds Success

Without feedback, people are often unaware of where they fall short and how they can improve. Without feedback, people stagnate. With feedback, they adjust and grow.

REFLECTIONS / PRACTICES

Now that you've read this chapter, think about or journal on the following questions:

- What other benefits of feedback come to mind while reading this?
- What benefit would you gain if you provided more feedback?
- What benefit would others gain if you provided more feedback?

With these new insights, who in your life are you ready to practice giving feedback to?

KEY TAKEAWAY

There are structured strategies that exist that can help to make effective feedback a regular feature of organizational development and improve company culture.

CHAPTER 3

The Cost of Not Giving Feedback

The single biggest problem in communication
is the illusion that it has taken place.

~George Bernard Shaw

As you can likely guess, it's obvious to most of my clients that I believe feedback is a positive and powerful tool used to enhance relationships and improve a company's bottom line. I was intrigued, then, when one day a client asked the perfect question, "What are the costs of not giving feedback?"

Given how busy we are with the day-to-day of our professional lives, we don't often pause to reflect on our relationship to feedback. This means we rarely look at the very real costs of not speaking up. Costs I have seen play out in myriad ways over the last twenty-five years. When we avoid giving feedback for whatever reason (fear, not enough time), everyone loses out. It turns out we also have an unconscious bias toward remaining silent rather than offering hard truths. So not giving feedback often feels like an easier choice, even though, as you'll see, it really isn't.

"If you can't say anything nice, don't say anything at all" was a favorite saying of my parents and teachers, and perhaps yours too. This adage established a belief in most of us that we are doing a "nice thing" by not providing constructive feedback or saying anything negative. Keeping quiet can seem like the most positive position to take. So why is it that it never works out quite the way we imagine?

There are ramifications to not sharing what's on our mind, that we are often blind to or choose to forget. When we need to speak out and don't, we may feel resentful or frustrated toward the person we should be talking to. Even when we don't put our feelings into words, we exude an underlying energy of "something being wrong." Everyone can see or feel "it," and no one is saying "it." Yes, the proverbial elephant in the room.

Most of us are brilliant at critiquing others without speaking directly to the person concerned. We gather around the watercooler or in small circles and gossip like mad. "Hey, Joe, did you see what she did in that meeting? Wow. I would have never presented information like that. I wonder if she knows how bad she did?" Or "He got it all wrong again. Doesn't he ever listen?" Or "She's not going to succeed if she doesn't stop talking over others." Of course, this kind of commentary can feel mildly satisfying to those providing it. The idea being that we are the enlightened ones who aren't making a mess of things. But how does it help the person being talked about? How does it help the team? The company? Easy answer: It doesn't. In fact, it tends to lead to cliques and divisiveness, which are counterproductive to individual and company success.

There's no blame here. As humans, we are equipped early on to notice negative situations and behaviors. We are much less equipped to directly address these situations and behaviors with the person who needs to know and who can do something with the information.

What do we do instead? We wait it out. Wish it away. Ignore it. We think one day they will see the light and mend their ways. We hope that someone else will tell them the cold hard truth. We become a little bit cowardly. In the end, we don't feel that great about ourselves—not addressing the problem weighs on us, whether we're conscious of it or not. And gossip only feels good in the moment.

Instead of absolving ourselves of responsibility or gossiping, we could confront the fact that not giving feedback can have a lasting and detrimental impact. I don't say this lightly. I've seen it happen, over and over again, and all too often.

Have you ever heard of the statement "By not making a decision, you're making a decision"? Well, by not providing feedback, you're providing feedback. And here's why I have no doubt about that.

———————

When I was in high school, my mother died, and at age 17 I was allowed to live in a small apartment of my own. While attending high school, I held a part-time job as a secretary in a law firm that was co-owned by my friend's father. RJ, a gifted attorney, was an easygoing and funny boss—patient and good at setting expectations. At first, I loved working for him and the other attorneys in the law firm. I was challenged with the work and loved what I was learning.

A few months in, RJ started putting his arm around me. It felt at first like fatherly affection. And then it didn't. One afternoon, exuberant from winning a big case, he pulled me into a full-on embrace. I didn't say anything. Not one, single word about feeling uncomfortable. I completed my day, not telling anyone what had happened, and the next day I called in sick. And the next I called in sick again. And again. I was lying, which I hated to do, but at the time it seemed easier than confronting the truth and saying how I felt and why I was quitting.

On Monday, I turned in my letter of resignation (without the requisite two weeks' notice) and left. RJ and his office manager called me a few times to find out what was wrong. I told them, "Nothing. I just can't work there anymore. Something else has come up."

———————————————

Flash forward to today. I have many more years of life experience, as well as experience facilitating hundreds of workshops for thousands of people, on topics ranging from interpersonal communications skills to harassment awareness training. Here's what I know now.

I should have said something to RJ early on about how I felt. I know that he felt protective of me in a fatherly kind of way, because my mother had died two years before. I was his daughter's friend, and I was parentless. What he didn't know is that his hugs were making me uncomfortable. More than that, by not speaking my truth, RJ didn't receive the needed lesson to "back off." It also took away my own power. I had to leave a job I loved because I was uncomfortable. I just didn't know how to say it out loud without feeling "weird" about it.

And yes, I was just seventeen years old. But still, when I go back and think about what happened, here's what I would have liked my young self to have said:

- "RJ, I want you to know that I am not comfortable with your hugs anymore and certainly not with an embrace. I don't like it. Can you honor my wishes and not hug me anymore?" And maybe I would have stayed in my job.

- Or "RJ, I've decided to quit my job as I am no longer comfortable working in an environment where a boss is putting his arm around my shoulders and has pulled me into an embrace. I find that totally inappropriate. Therefore, I'm quitting without notice."

- Or "RJ, don't hug me. I don't like it."

Even thinking about these different scenarios makes me feel more powerful. Stuffing down my feelings—and feedback—hurt me for several years. And my bet, even if the circumstances weren't as extreme as mine, you can probably think of times when you wish you'd spoken out. Like when a boss was rude to you, or a colleague slighted you during a meeting, or when your new employee didn't return your emails, or the woman in the next cubicle ate odorous popcorn all day long. And you said nothing. And they didn't change. And you didn't grow, except in resentment, and even felt a little less powerful every day.

THOUGHTS ON FEEDBACK

**Failure to give feedback can be bad for
your health and your peace of mind.**

When people avoid giving critical feedback, they feel anxiety and stress and build up the situation disproportionately in their minds. The stories get bigger and scarier. People lose sleep over things unsaid.

THE FINANCIAL COST

Shari Harley, an expert in feedback, has a 2014 video that describes a practice manager who kept stripping away responsibilities from an employee who was underperforming until there wasn't much of the job left. When Shari asked the practice manager how long this had been going on, she replied, "Four years." When Shari asked the practice manager why she hadn't said anything, the practice manager said, "I really like her and providing her with feedback is hard."

This is a common story among managers. It goes like this:

- He/she is a good person.
- Everyone likes [name of employee].
- He/she isn't great at the job but they are popular, fun, and likable.
- I can't possibly let [name of employee] go. Everyone will be devastated.

I get it that giving honest feedback to someone you like is often harder than providing it to someone you don't feel kindly toward. But take a moment to consider how lack of feedback can impact the finances of an organization. Saying nothing means no change. And certainly no change in results.

In 2021, according to the Bureau of Labor Statistics, the national average wage index was $60,575.07. For simple math purposes, let's say this employee was making $60,000/year. Four years of not saying anything means that this company spent $240,000 for an unproductive yet likable employee. Sign me up for that job! Even if their salary was far less, even say $7.25/hour or $15,080 per year, which is the federally mandated minimum wage, over four years it is still $60,000 that was misspent on an under- or non-performer. Regardless of how you look at it, there is an actual financial cost in not saying anything. And this is for one employee. What if this practice manager was managing three or four ineffective employees? It happens all the time.

The direct financial consequence of paying a salary for a job not being done well is only one element of the financial cost of keeping quiet. Not only is the company paying an employee to not complete their work, but also the offset of that employee's workload can impact the performance of other team members or you as a manager. This cost is less measurable, but surely still has a considerable financial impact on the company.

Generally, what tends to happen when one team member is underperforming is that others on the team are required to pick up the slack, and often without pay or recognition. This can have devastating impacts on overall morale. An employee may not be doing their job but someone is, as I am quick to tell my clients. And it might just be you.

"I am so mad at this employee. Why can't he get the job done right? I give him the task, and the result is wrong. I explain what I want, and it still isn't getting done correctly. I end up taking it away and doing it myself. This keeps happening. Why can't the employee just figure it out?!" As I listened to my client "vent," it was clear that the person's frustration had little to do with the employee and more to do with their own inability to hold the employee accountable. Sound familiar? Let's face it, most of us have fallen into the trap of "training" our co-workers or employees by not saying anything and then simply doing the task ourselves.

Worse still is when an employee is tossed the responsibility of an underperforming peer, adding to their burdens, without compensating them. You can see what a bad message this sends to everyone. To the underperforming employee, "I don't need to work hard; I just need to get on the right side of the boss." And for the employee who was burdened with the extra work, "My co-worker is a jerk, and my boss is clueless. No one appreciates the fact that I am doing two people's jobs. Why do I have to do that employee's work?" The entire team is thinking, "Yeah, that employee is cool and all, but I'm not loving the fact that the person isn't doing their fair share."

When a manager unconsciously enables an employee's lack of performance, there is a detrimental impact on other employees and the organization. This unintentional co-opted relationship will continue to erode productivity and goodwill until something changes.

REFLECTIONS / PRACTICES

Let's pause here for a moment to reflect on a time when you said nothing about a performance issue at work. Pull out your notepad and jot a few things down. Remember, this is your chance to reflect on your own experiences so that you can identify what you want to practice improving.

What was holding you back from saying anything? Look deep. For example, "I don't want to upset the person." "The person is a nice person." "I'm afraid I'll say the wrong thing." "This person won't be able to handle the feedback."

What did you gain by not saying anything? For example, "I didn't rock the boat." "I didn't upset that person." "I kept that relationship intact."

What did you lose by not saying anything? For example, "Time." "Productivity." "Quality." "Sleep."

Ancillary Financial Costs

In the early 2000s, I was asked by a COO I reported to to pull together a severance package for Cindy, a high-level marketing executive who had been employed with our company for a year. I wasn't surprised by the request as I knew Cindy wasn't doing a satisfactory job. There had been several missed deadlines and subpar work. I also knew that no one on the leadership team had followed my recommendations to provide her with direct feedback. When I asked the COO about the quick shift to a severance package rather than offering specific performance feedback, his response was, "We don't have time for that. I'd like to provide her with half of her annual salary as her severance. Let's get the package together and get her out of here by the end of the week."

I shared with the COO that I believed the organization was taking a risk by not documenting and sharing the specific performance issue with the employee. The employee was female, was over forty, and had recently shared that she needed to take family medical leave. I also mentioned that if we pulled a package together under the umbrella of position elimination, it would pose a risk of not being able to replace her for up to a year. The COO said that he didn't care what type of risk it would pose and to handle it as swiftly as possible. "I've heard your recommendation," he told me. "I've considered the risks and I'm asking you to do it. Now."

I documented the conversation with the COO and, as requested, pulled together the package. When the COO and I presented the details for the position elimination and shared the Separation Agreement, Cindy expressed both surprise and anger. She told us she felt as though she wasn't treated fairly or with dignity and believed she was targeted. She planned to speak with her attorney.

Cindy did just that, and while no discriminatory action was found to have occurred, the company, in addition to paying out a hefty severance package, was caught up in costly and time-consuming litigation.

The truth is the organization could have saved a lot of time and expense if feedback on Cindy's performance had been clearly and regularly stated and documented from the start of her employment. This is one of a hundred similar stories I could tell. Each organization has its own set of practices; however, I would *always* encourage that if a performance issue exists that the employee be made aware of the situation. Not only will this avoid potential litigation down the line, but it is the right thing to do. Most people have the desire and the capability to change and grow from feedback. A struggling employee can become a powerful asset. And even if you don't keep them on, your feedback may help them to level up their game in their next job.

Human "Disengagement" Cost

Over the seven years of managing a customer service team for a medium-sized business, Peter was able to take advantage of several development opportunities. The most recent was a six-month emerging leaders' program that felt perfectly timed. Peter was working hard to improve his leadership skills to move into the next available director position. His manager and others in the organization were aware of Peter's ambition and fully supported this next step. Within three months of graduating from the emerging leader's program, a director position opened at the company. Peter immediately notified his manager of his desire to apply and received wholehearted support.

After a series of interviews and what appeared to be "positive" indicators, Peter called me, distraught. Not only did he not get the promotion, but the hiring manager also didn't contact Peter directly. Instead, an announcement of the new director was made to the entire organization. To make matters worse, Peter was the one to initiate a conversation with the hiring manager asking for feedback as to why he'd been overlooked. The unsatisfactory answer was: "I don't believe you could perform the position. I decided to select the best candidate for the role. Better luck next time, Peter."

Absent of any concrete feedback, Peter wondered how he could improve his leadership skills for the next opportunity, when he had no idea of where he fell short. How could he even think of re-applying should another opening occur, if he had no idea what he was supposed to do differently? This was a no-win situation. It was no surprise to me when Peter, who was considered "valuable," resigned his position within two months. He moved to a new company in a director role with a 40 percent increase in pay. Good for Peter. Not so good for the company, who had invested in, trained, and developed him for seven years, and then essentially lost him because they didn't tell him why he hadn't been chosen for the next-level position.

It's easy to see how this situation impacted Peter. It's also important to recognize that his peers were aware of how Peter was treated through the process. Naturally, Peter shared some of his grievances. And more importantly, if Peter felt he was being groomed for the job, others would have felt the same. When he was overlooked, it would be natural for others to become skeptical about the internal career and promotion process. If leaders could not be trusted to provide direct feedback on critical qualifications or development skills needed to achieve high-level leadership roles, who could?!

This scenario is an example of a career path gone awry. Peter no longer had a positive experience to share with others about how he was treated within the organization prior to his departure. And his departure can be directly correlated to the "miscommunication" and lack of meaningful feedback from a member of the leadership team.

REFLECTIONS / PRACTICES

As you consider this story and the associated costs, reflect on what you have learned. Then write down what you would do if you were Peter, the hiring manager, or Peter's manager.

For purposes of this exercise, practice providing feedback from all angles:

- Peter: What feedback would you provide to the hiring manager? To your current manager?
- Peter's Manager: What feedback would provide to the hiring manager? To Peter?
- Hiring Manager: What feedback would you provide to Peter? To Peter's manager?

Cost of "Limited" Development and Employee Departure

Jayne had been performing in a director-level position for five years when a VP position opened in her department. After applying and interviewing with several members on the executive team, she learned from her direct manager that she didn't receive the promotion, but that her male counterpart had. Her manager told Jayne, "Here's the reason, Jayne. Your presentation skills need improvement; you use twenty words where you could use five."

Jayne told me she was literally reeling from shock at hearing this. Before she could stop herself, she said to her boss, "What? I've never heard this before. I've been in my role for five years, have done count-less presentations to hundreds of people, including you, and I have never heard this feedback before now.

"If this was so important to my success, why wasn't it ever brought up in a performance evaluation? Why haven't you suggested that I attend a course or get coaching on my presentation skills? You've never indicated that my lack of presentation skills or use of words would prohibit me from continued career growth. Never." Jayne told me that her manager apologized while looking at his desk and didn't look up again as she left his office.

Jayne spent a few minutes reflecting on her experience after relaying it back to me, and then told me, "Throughout our working relationship, my manager never provided constructive criticism about my presen-tation skills. We even traveled across the country giving presentations together. The only feedback I received was 'Great job!' or 'That went well!'"

Jayne felt betrayed, deflated, undermined, and undervalued. She was open to the fact that she had room for improvement, but Jayne's trust in her immediate manager and her peers was instantaneously eroded. Years of shared experiences had not resulted in feedback that could have resulted in a promotion. After that conflict with her boss, he took Jayne out to lunch to provide further coaching on the matter. It did make Jayne think about how she could improve; however, at that time, it was too little too late. Not long after, Jayne found a new opportunity outside of the organization where she thrives as a sought-after and admired presenter and facilitator in her field. Jayne could have continued with her old company, if they'd offered the feedback she needed to thrive and grow. But apparently they didn't. And that was their loss.

But let's put ourselves in Jayne's manager's shoes for a moment. Perhaps he was surprised by what she said to him. Hadn't he told her on that Uber ride after the meeting that her presentation had run a little over? Or what about when they were walking to lunch together one day; hadn't he casually brought up the topic of keeping to the PowerPoint? Thinking back, it may have been that Jayne wasn't paying attention to what he was saying in the moment. Hadn't she responded strangely to his feedback about going over time by saying, "But it went great, didn't it? I mean, they loved it!" And he'd felt the need to give her a little praise too, so he'd said, "You did a great job, as always. Just try and keep to the script next time." And maybe that's all Jayne heard: "You did a great job." Then she was on to reading her texts, thinking about picking her kids up from school, and everything else.

This scenario plays out a thousand different ways in a thousand different organizations every day. Feedback is offered on the go—in an Uber, a bar, walking between meetings, and/or in the moment without the intended recipient's full attention. This often means the message isn't received. The giver of feedback may feel, "Well, that's a relief, I said what I needed to say." But did they? Bottom line, feedback isn't feedback until it's been received by the person to whom it is delivered. It's useless if it isn't framed clearly or forcefully enough to register. Trying to be subtle with feedback is like whispering at a long distance and hoping someone hears you. It just doesn't work.

REFLECTIONS / PRACTICES

Practice: Places

Name some of the places you've given feedback. Consider how these places or occasions supported the feedback. Did the other person receive your feedback? How do you know? Did you follow up afterward? Were you each clear about what was being said and what each person was responsible for making happen?

Practice: Getting Clear

Can you think of any recent situations where you needed to provide feedback to a leader, a peer, or a direct report where you may have "wimped out" or "wedged the feedback" into a friendly conversation? If so, pause here.

I invite you to grab your tablet, computer, or favorite writing tool and pad and write down the following:

- The name of the person.
- The situation. Where it was, when it happened, what it was.
- The behavior. Describe for yourself the specific behavior that is getting in the way of the person's success.
- The impact. What is the impact of the specific behavior? Why is that important? And why now?
- What needs to be changed and what happens if it doesn't?

Is this a conversation you can broach now? If so, schedule the time and make it happen. This is an important practice to get into. Create time, space, and structure for the conversation, and have compassion for yourself as you head into what can feel like a tough situation. You will be better for the experience. And so will the person you need to share the information with.

The Company Culture Cost

I am often tasked with conducting follow-up or exit interviews with employees who are leaving or have left an organization. This is to discern if there are certain trends or reasons that result in employee attrition that need to be considered and for changes to be made with organizational practices. I am typically asked to ascertain the reason for leaving and the overall experiences at the company. In cases like these, the questions asked are the same for each person, so that the data gathered can be consolidated into themes that may reveal the complete picture.

A steady trickle of resignations in a very short period left a client devastated. He asked that I follow up with everyone who'd left to understand why. After conducting exit interviews, a clear picture emerged. Employees consistently reported being unsure about the direction of the organization, and even who was in charge. In their words, the organization felt too unstructured; too informal; too chaotic. Who's really in charge?

I asked each employee, "Have you shared these concerns with your manager or anyone else in the organization?"

Each employee said something to the effect of, "No, I'm too uncomfortable with doing that. Don't get me wrong, I really like the company and what they do. I just don't like the lack of vision or leadership structure. Without that, I feel lost and confused and have decided to work for a company that has clarity about who's in charge and where they are headed. I thought I could work in a company that was a bit 'loose' with policies and structure and stuff, and now I know it doesn't work for me."

Wow. A treasure trove of information, and now I was to share it with the CEO. This was going to be interesting.

In preparing for the meeting, I reflected on the fact that while I understood its policies and services, I was not as familiar with the mission of the organization. I also realized that I didn't fully understand how they went about their day-to-day decision-making and communications.

When I laid out the results of the exit interviews with the CEO, he was quiet. Then he took a deep breath and asked for time to process the information or feedback. We would continue our meeting the next day.

Having had time to distill the comments, the CEO had realized the underlying problem by the time we met the following morning. He had created the idea for the company and hired some very smart and creative people he hoped would organically and collaboratively co-create a clear vision and path for the organization. Only, the people he hired wanted his leadership and a pre-determined structure. They wanted someone to lead the pack, guiding them on the trail toward a common goal. And the CEO felt he couldn't do this yet because didn't have an explicit vision.

As a result of our conversation, the CEO set out two possible paths for himself. One, to work with a strong business coach to explore and articulate his vision, strategy, and the structure needed to achieve his goals. Only then would he hire the right people to implement it. Second, that he start by hiring people specifically to work with him on the ideation of the organization. At the end of the day, the CEO chose the first path as it was more direct and less expensive, and it allowed him to reach his goals sooner.

While the feedback wasn't communicated directly from employees to the CEO, the indirect manner in providing the feedback to me as a consultant, and my findings from the exit interviews, helped the CEO to understand what was missing and to get back on the right path.

As a leader you will sometimes receive direct feedback from your employees if they feel safe enough to be honest with you. But it's also helpful to create a system of feedback through an outside consultant. The value of working with someone like me is that it provides your employees with a third party they may feel safer confiding in. As well, a consultant can provide the objectivity often needed to observe and articulate what's really going on.

The Emotional Cost of Withholding Feedback

A friend's son (we'll call him Jack) was attending college and working part-time for a small franchise organization. When he first started his job, he was excited and engaged. The agreed upon thirty-two hours per week was ideal for his schedule and met his financial needs. After about eight weeks, however, he noticed that his hours were being cut back week by week until by the ninth week of work he was down to twenty-five hours. He asked several times to speak with his manager about it, but his manager was always "too busy" to talk. Jack quit his job at week thirteen, by which time his hours were almost cut in half. When he gave his notice, his manager acted surprised. "What's up, man? I thought you liked it here."

Jack said, "I do like it here. But I wasn't getting the hours I needed and that we agreed upon. I just figured that I wasn't either liked here or wasn't doing my job. Every time I tried to talk to you about it, you were too busy. I've been racking my brain and have gotten pretty upset over the past few weeks that you weren't available to take the time to let me know what was going on. I had a few sleepless nights trying to figure it out and finally decided that I wasn't what you needed."

His manager asked Jack to stay.

But Jack had the maturity to set his own boundary, telling the manager, "I've decided to work for an organization and a boss who appreciates the work I do and respects me enough to take the time to talk with me when things change or when I need to do something different. I'm out of here. Good luck, man."

When agreements or expectations change such as fewer hours, less responsibility, or less access to our managers, for example—and we aren't told why—we make up a story about it. Our human brains unconsciously fill in the blanks to make sense of things. A few stories that I've heard over the years when employees don't hear directly from their leaders go like this:

- "I'm not doing my job, and no one wants to tell me."
- "They don't like me here."
- "They're trying to tell me something and it's probably not good."
- "He/she (the boss) is a jerk (or worse)."
- "He/she thinks they are too good to respond to me."

People tend to make assumptions based on past experiences or insecurities, creating stories that are untrue and not reassuring. The fact is, these stories feel true enough to influence our actions and decision making, until and unless direct input or feedback is provided by the other party.

The moral of Jack's story is this: If you want to retain talent and keep your workers engaged and loyal, then let them know what's going on and make time to have "the talk" rather than running from it and allowing your employees to create their own stories.

Cost of Trust in Work Relationships

Sami, an acquaintance of mine, called me crying after she was let go on a Friday afternoon.

"Joni, I didn't know who else to call. I feel so upset and don't know where to turn."

"Sami, I'm right here," I responded. "If you can, please give me a few minutes. I'm in the middle of something and I need to finish it up. I'll call you back in five minutes so that I can be fully present with you. Can you do this?"

Sami said, "Yes, please. I'll be here."

I called Sami back in five minutes as promised and she launched into the following story.

———————

After a full day of work, Sami's boss called her in and said, "Sami, today is your last day. We won't need you to return next week."

Sami was stunned. She'd been working for the organization for eighteen months and believed she had a good relationship with her peers and boss. "What? What do you mean this is my last day?"

"Your contributions and performance aren't where they need to be, and we are letting you go immediately."

"You've never said anything to me about my lack of performance or problems with my contributions. Why am I not receiving a warning of some sort? Shouldn't I have heard about this before now so that I could adjust?"

According to Sami, without even a hint of apology or compassion, her boss responded, "Some organizations might do that. We don't. If an employee isn't working out, we let the employee go. You seem like a nice person. I didn't want to hurt your feelings or make you feel bad about yourself by telling you that you weren't performing as expected."

Now truly stressed, Sami asked, "What about my feelings now? I feel like the rug has just been pulled out from underneath my feet. I just leased a new apartment and bought new furniture. You know that. I've been telling you about this for weeks. Why didn't you say something before I put myself more in debt? You were excited for my new place. And now, I feel like I've been punched in the gut. This is a terrible thing to do to a person."

Sami's boss said, "I'm sorry you feel this way. Would you like me to help you gather your belongings?"

Shortly after that, Sami calls me. After listening and allowing Sami to share what she is feeling, what I am certain of is that this experience will trail Sami into any new job she holds. She won't know who to trust or when to trust. It will likely take Sami a while to fully give her best to a future employer.

Regardless organizational practice or policy, I believe the way Sami was notified of her termination was unprofessional and damaging.

Put yourself in Sami's position. You're performing in a job and feeling good about your contributions. You work for an organization that you like and with people whom you feel an affinity toward. Each day that you wake up, you know that you are providing value, and you don't feel a lot of stress in your work life. You feel so comfortable that you look to your future, leasing a new apartment, purchasing new furniture. You are settling into your role and your life.

And in a moment, your life turns upside down. No signs. No warning. Bam. Let go. Terminated. Performance issues. F-I-R-E-D. By someone you once trusted and don't any longer.

It's hard to imagine what Sami went through that day. And yet, Sami's situation is sadly not that unusual in the workplace. So, this begs the question: Even if you are legally able to fire someone without warning or explanation, should you? What might have been different if her boss had provided performance feedback to Sami months beforehand? Would she have found out how she might improve? Or would she have simply been put on notice that her employment was not secure, and so refrained from taking on a lease for a new and more expensive apartment? Who can say? But one thing is certain, Sami would never forget this experience. And all because she was never given the feedback that she was failing. She was simply let go.

When we as leaders get in the habit of avoiding feedback, we run the risk of becoming unapproachable or even callous, as the stories of Jack and Sami show. We signal that we don't care enough about our employees to take time to respond to questions or offer constructive criticism or warranted recognition. But something else happens as well. Members of the organization (ourselves included) run the risk of becoming impervious to criticism, assuming the stance of "I (or the company) can do no wrong." In the process, we allow ourselves or others to operate without course correction. We don't integrate changes and grow. Lack of feedback isn't just the absence of something; it creates the risk of doing measurable harm.

Cost of Toxic Environments

An organization had set high levels of expectations for sales revenues. One of their best sales employees happened to be a "bear" to work with. While she had a remarkable sales track record, she berated her co-workers, badmouthed her boss, gossiped about her customers, and behaved in unethical ways to "get the sale done." This salesperson was driven to be number one at all costs. She didn't care who she stepped on or kicked out of the way to maintain her position of top salesperson. The company told her to deliver results and so she did.

Her co-workers brought her behavior to the attention of their boss. They were honest about the demoralizing effect she was having on the team. The boss dismissed the feedback and said, "When you achieve her level of sales we can talk about her behavior." His message was clear: "Back off. We have a good thing going here and I'm not going to disturb it." The other message was, "I am going to allow the behavior, because we are exceeding financial expectations, no matter what the cost is to you."

The employees who complained to the boss chose to leave the organization and filed a charge against the boss and the company for hostile work environment harassment. The charge was found in favor *of the employees. The high sales revenue created for the organization by its toxic employee ended up paying for attorney and settlement fees. Who wins in this case?*

The bottom line is this: There are more risks and costs associated with not giving feedback than giving it. Case in point: Failing to offer feedback to an employee who is behaving in an unprofessional or unethical manner may cost you an arm and a lawsuit.

THOUGHTS ON FEEDBACK

We All Have Blind Spots

We don't know how we are experienced by others, unless someone shares something they see in us. It sometimes requires others to shine a light in areas we can't see ourselves.

Imagine you've had lunch with a friend where you enjoyed a delicious salad and connecting conversation. After lunch, you head to a meeting with a group of co-workers. You step into the restroom after the meeting, and while washing your hands you look up into the mirror above the faucet, smile, and notice you have a big piece of lettuce stuck in your teeth. Ugh. Why didn't anyone say anything? What is the cost to you when the people you care about and work with don't say anything? How does that make you feel?

This chapter offered several different examples of the costs of not providing feedback. What examples have you experienced in your own life related to the cost of either not giving feedback or not receiving feedback? The costs sometimes are too many to add up. My hope is that this chapter has led you to consider who you want to be in the realm of being a great leader.

REFLECTIONS / PRACTICES

Think about someone you work with as a boss, direct report, or peer. Is there any feedback that you've been withholding? Anything at all?

- Dig deep. Even the smallest things may need the smallest feedback.

- Start with a simple opening:
  - » I've noticed that there is something you do that you might want to know about. Would you mind if I shared it with you?
  - » I've been meaning to tell you something that I've noticed. Is now a good time?

- Articulate exactly what it is. It could be as simple as the examples below:
  - » You always say "awesome." There are other words you could use that would help (fill in the blank). *I personally received this from one of my direct reports.*
  - » I wanted to let you know that I appreciate it when you double-check my calculations. While it's hard for me to accept when my work isn't 100 percent accurate, I'd rather we work together as a team to produce accurate information. Thank you for that. *I received this from one of my peers.*
  - » The fonts, font sizes, and formatting in your presentations isn't consistent. I noticed a few words were

misspelled too. I think you would have better engagement if you corrected those items before presenting
to an audience. *I provided this to my boss.*

- There are more nuanced examples too.
  » Are you asking me those questions because you're
    interested in my perspective or because you want me
    to tell you what you want to hear? *Feedback I provided
    to a boss. After I provided him the feedback, he realized
    he wanted me to agree with him at first, but over time
    became interested in my perspective.*
  » In reviewing your accounting, I noticed that you've had
    several oversights with your invoicing. You could write
    it off for the third time this year. Or, we can go to the
    customer, admit our error, and you can add money to
    your income this year. *A friend said to her boss.*

Now that you've practiced some opening feedback remarks and
seen some examples of what feedback can look like, it's time to try
it out for yourself. The following prompts are meant to inspire you
to provide feedback in a purposeful, caring, connected, and meaningful way.

- **Is there someone in your professional life today that would
  benefit from feedback?** Write down the person's name and the
  nature of the feedback. For example, "I need to give feedback
  to John. The nature of the feedback is to let him know that it's
  important to me that he updates our agreed-upon task list in
  our project management system before each day ends. This is
  important to me so that I can see where we are at each stage
  of the project to prepare for my client meetings the next day."

Providing feedback can be "too hard" to some, and often it's because of **our fear** of what to say, what they'll say, and/or how they will react. When fear is present, we lose sight of the larger purpose for the feedback. When preparing to provide feedback, frame it out for yourself this way:

- **What is the purpose of the feedback?** For example, "To improve performance." "To change a behavior."

- **How will the feedback help the person I am providing it to?** For example, "They will know specifically what performance I am looking for." "They will know what behavior needs to change and will therefore have the opportunity to make that change."

- **How will the feedback help me, the team, the organization, our customers?** For example, "If giving feedback is hard for me, I will grow through the experience." "If the person chooses to improve performance/behavior, the team will benefit."

- **What is stopping me from giving critical feedback?** For example, "I don't want to hurt the person's feelings." "I don't know what to say."

- **What is the worst-case scenario of giving feedback?** For example, "I won't be able to control the outcome." "The person might get upset; how would I handle that?"

- **What is the best-case scenario of giving feedback?** For example, "The person is relieved to have the issue brought to light and the offer of support to improve."

Once you've written all of this out, what do you notice now? Will you give feedback to that person? If so, by when?

KEY TAKEAWAY

The risks to your organization of not providing feedback affects the bottom line, employee retention, and company morale. In fact, every area of your business may be negatively impacted by lack of feedback.

CHAPTER 4

How Energy Is a Form of Feedback

Life is about the management of energy.
Where you place your attention,
you place your energy.

~Joe Dispenza

The Path of Least Effort

I was meeting with a long-term client who held a C-level position at an emerging technology organization and could see he was extremely agitated. His jaw clenched; he almost spat his words out when talking about a peer with whom he was having a challenging time. While I was settling into my chair, I took in his anxious pacing, fast speech, and shaking voice. He was barely able to catch his breath. His neck muscles tensed up and his face flushed as he shared the situation with me. This was the first time in my two years of working with this client that I had seen him like this.

After about ten minutes of him spewing details regarding the situation, he just stopped. He sat down at his desk, took a deep breath in, and exhaled while dropping his head in his hands, rubbing his forehead, and at the same time shaking his head. As he took a few more breaths, I said, "Wow. That was a lot of information in a short period of time."

He said, "I guess I've been bottling it up for a while. I knew that my peer was frustrating me, but not this much." He laughed and said a bit shakily, "I didn't see this coming."

I said, "What's going on? What didn't you see?"

He said, "That I've let this knucklehead get under my skin so much. He's a jerk and a bully. I feel like I need to shake it off and go for a run. That should put me back to being clear-minded about the situation and not so hot-headed."

I looked at him, chuckled, and said, "So that's what you see? A good run should take care of all of this. Is that really it?"

He stood up, looked out his office window, and as he turned back to look at me, he shrugged his shoulders a bit like a small child might do, looked at the floor with his hands in his pockets, and said, "I just don't know what to do."

I asked him, "What would you like to do?"

He said, "I'd like to tell him exactly how I feel."

I asked, "Why don't you?"

My client's head popped up for a moment. And then his head dropped. Then in a defeated way, he quietly said, "I could never do that. I just don't have it in me. It's just easier to let the situation go."

"It's just easier to let it go." I hear those words a lot from leaders across organizations today. Perhaps, like me, you sense the resignation or defeat that accompanies such a response. And that's what I want to focus on. The energy behind the words.

One aspect of energy is that of least effort. In fact, the Principle of Least Effort was defined in 1894 by Italian philosopher Guillaume Ferrero in an article in the *Revue philosophique de la France et de l'étranger*. The article stated that when deciding between two options, people will naturally gravitate toward the option that requires the least amount of work. For example, while studying, you might think, "Why read the whole book if a crib sheet is available?" If you're information gathering, you might think, "Why conduct research in a library when a YouTube video is out there to be seen?" And yes, it also happens when you think, "Why give feedback and face a possible confrontation when you can just let it go?"

There are, of course, many reasons it would be a bad thing to always take the shortcut or easy way out. Goodness knows, we don't rely on people or want to work with those who never delve deeply into anything. But why is the easy way also detrimental in the case of feedback? After all, aren't there times when it is good to just let things go? Won't the situation just work itself out? Doesn't it always work out in the end?

There are times for "letting it go." But in this situation, as mentioned above with my irate client, and many other clients and partners I've worked with over the years, not every situation is one of those times. And here's why. Merely "letting it go" won't do anything for my client. His upset won't just vanish. It will remain deeply situated in his mind and body. And experience tells me he will continue to relive this negative event and the destruction of the relationship by sharing it with family, friends, and co-workers. Regardless of how many times he tells the story, the tension he feels about his co-worker and the situation will not budge. Until he does something about it—in the form of providing honest feedback to his colleague—the tension will continue to fuel his outbursts and raise his blood pressure, negatively impacting both his mind and body.

Offering feedback can provide the outlet needed to release that tension. Once we honestly express our feelings and concerns, whatever the outcome, we free ourselves from the negative energy loop that keeps us trapped. The way to let "it" go is to share the information with the person who can do something about it. In other words,

"The truth will set you free," so long as you offer it to the right person and in the right way.

Owning Your Full Spectrum Energy

Let's back up for a minute and add some context to the word *energy* in relation to feedback. I've learned over the years that there is a range of energy, from stressed out to calm (and everything in between), that shows up in our mind, body, emotions, and belief systems. Energy is something that lives within us and is experienced outside of ourselves by those around us. Energy can shift quickly and frequently. Think about energy like you would weather.

On a beautiful sunny day in May, while living in Denver, my youngest daughter had a soccer game at 10:00 a.m. It was 70 degrees and simply gorgeous. Everyone was happy that the "worst of the winter" was behind us, and we were looking forward to a beautiful spring and summer. I opened all the windows in the house to let the fresh air in. Around 3 p.m., we drove to the airport to drop someone off. The airport was twenty-seven miles away or approximately thirty-five minutes. When we left our house, it was 70 degrees. Halfway to the airport, we noticed that the temperature had dropped to 50 degrees, and it was raining. When we were five miles from the airport, snowflakes were falling and the weather was 36 degrees. Just like that, the weather unexpectedly and drastically shifted. And when I arrived home, there was snow inside of my house—gusting through those open windows.

While none of us can control the weather, we can manage our energy. Indeed, when it comes to offering feedback, being able to recognize the energy you are giving off, and how it shifts from moment to moment, it is key to becoming a feedback expert.

Recall the opening story of this chapter. My client's energy began as red-hot anger, and then turned into resignation, then defeat, deflation, and finally exhaustion. This describes one side of the energy feedback spectrum, often associated with the Principle of Least Effort. We simply don't have it in us to step up to the moment and respond effectively. The more we follow the aspect of Least Effort, the more we create deep grooves in our memories, emotions, and bodies about "that person" who that did "that thing" that triggered me and made me frustrated, angry, worthless, etc. Relationships veer off track when we lean into this energy. Paradoxically, by not confronting someone (Least Effort) our feelings, energy, and relationship separation require a greater expense of energy, ending up costing us More Effort.

I've created a color-coded spectrum (Figure 3) to illustrate how broad of a range our energy fields can flow through.

FIGURE 3

The feeling of defeat lies somewhere in the middle of the energy spectrum. Anger and resentment, however, hang out in the stress section (imagine seeing red—the left side). This section is activated when the amygdala gets hijacked and prompts the sympathetic part of the nervous system to create a fight, flight, or freeze response. When this happens, you absolutely cannot think clearly, so you react from a heated sense of anger and frustration, or you may feel the desire to run away, find yourself paralyzed, or even end up flattering the person you meant to admonish. I've done all of these on occasion, and believe me, it only creates deeper problems down the road.

The other side of the energy spectrum (the imagine seeing green—the right side) is a more relaxed response, in which the parasympathetic system acts to inhibit the body from overworking, creating a calmer, more creative, open, and connected space. This is the part that wants to engage, find solutions, and thrive. This is Marc telling me that saying "Yes" to everything isn't working. It's me being able to stand up to a boss and say, "I don't want to be a part of this—what can we do to make the situation better?" It's a leadership group saying, "You know what, we have been cussing inappropriately—it's time we grew up." This is a dynamic place to be, and it's where change happens—because we are relaxed enough to open to new possibilities.

In between the two (stress and relaxed) is the middle or in-between state (imagine seeing yellow). This is what I would describe as "limbo;" not bad, not good, just "meh"—perhaps distracted, resigned, or defeated. It could represent a pause, a place of inaction and inertia. While the "limbo" state can be a comfortable place to hang out because nothing much happens here, it also represents a state of non-action. There's something comfortable about this space, but it changes nothing. We don't blow up and get mad or work to make up and create a new relationship. It's the same old same-old. And in my experience, this is the place most of us choose to hang out. And then we wonder why things aren't improving.

Energy matters. And it matters much more than we've been taught to believe.

How Our Energy Influences Feedback

If you come into a meeting highly stressed out, the energy you emit will magnetize the same energy back. It's the law of attraction; or simply, like attracts like. So, if you snap, they'll snap. If you are calm and open, they'll be calm and open. Your energy communicates more than your words do. It matters that you connect with yourself and check where you fall on the energy spectrum before you offer feedback.

One of the first advocates for the power of nonverbal communication was the renowned behavioral psychologist Dr. Albert Mehrabian. Mehrabian's extensive research on the topic of body language resulted in the 7-38-55 rule. The 7-38-55 rule indicates that only 7 percent of what we communicate is done verbally. The nonverbal, or energetic, component of our daily communication, meaning the tonality of our voice and body language, make up 38 percent and 55 percent respectively. Our tone of voice and our body language emanate something energetically that other people not only feel but also receive messaging from.

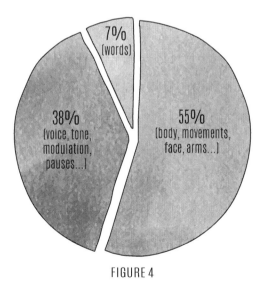

FIGURE 4

So, imagine that on the energy spectrum we previously touched on, you fall left of center (red or orangish) in what is called the "stress response or red zone" and you are readying to give feedback to a colleague or employee. Can you see how staying in that energy field would threaten your ability to connect? What if you move away from that feeling to a more relaxed state of mind where you are curious about and have a desire to connect with the person you are providing feedback to? Can you feel the difference in your body? Can you feel what a difference it might make to what you say, how you say it, and, most importantly, how it will land with the other person?

Ask yourself: *What do I want the person you are giving feedback to be left with after the conversation is complete?* Feedback should be part of helping someone grow or make a positive change. But if your energy shames or blames another, people won't hear what you have to say. They will react from a fight, flight, freeze, or fawn response, and the feedback will be lost.

In the early 2000s, I had two young daughters at home. Due to our blended family, the girls were shuttled back and forth between our house and their other parents' homes. My husband traveled for his job for over half of each year. Every holiday season between November and February, my mother-in-law and her partner came to visit us in Colorado. At that time, I held a high-pressure, senior, corporate role that involved occasional travel. I was also going to school part-time. Making it all work was extremely challenging, as you might imagine.

It was the week before Christmas and my mother-in-law, her partner, and their two full-size collie dogs were visiting. Snow was dumping at our house. My husband was taking his last business trip of the year in sunny California. On my way home from work, I stopped at the grocery store to pick up a few things to add to our dinner menu and proceeded to slip-slide home, arriving around 6:30 p.m. to a driveway covered in snow. I cautiously pulled into the garage, took a deep breath, and said a few silent prayers that my house wouldn't be too chaotic. As I walked through the door, the collies were barking, the girls were screaming and chasing each other through the house, my in-laws were watching the news, and the sink was full of breakfast dishes. I looked around and immediately felt my body tense and flush hot with negative energy and red-zone reactions. I was so far to the left of the energy spectrum, I almost needed another category.

I dropped my briefcase on the floor with a big bang and loudly deposited the groceries on the counter. The loud noises coupled with the furious (and somewhat victim) energy my body was emitting stopped everyone in their tracks. The girls paused and looked at each other with the "uh-oh" look (you know that one) and my mother-in-law rushed in to say, "Hi, honey! You look so tired. Is there anything I can help you with?"

I gritted my teeth. "No. Thank you. I'm fine. Just let me get settled here before I wash the dishes and get dinner going."

Mom looked sideways at her partner and then in her sing-songy voice gaily said, "Okay, honey, we'll clear out of here while you get everything cleaned up. Come on, girls . . ."

And everyone cleared out. Who could blame them? Truth be told, I wasn't "fine." I was furious and resentful that my in-laws hadn't washed the dishes from breakfast and that they were having all of the fun with the girls while I was working, shopping for groceries for dinner, and driving through the snow to a house that hadn't been shoveled yet, knowing that the snow would soon turn to ice. On top of that, I would be making dinner. Because, well, it seemed that on top of everything, I wasn't very good at asking for help.

As I sunk my hands into the warm, soapy bubbles and washed the dishes, I immediately felt a shift in my stress. The warm water began to calm me and I took some deep breaths. I closed my eyes and thought through what had just happened. What I really wanted was to return to a calm home where the kitchen was ready for dinner preparations, a fire was lit in the fireplace, and the girls had been bathed and readied *for bed so that after dinner we could read stories together. I relaxed into the familiarity of doing dishes, reflecting that there were two ways to move forward with this:*

- *One, I could have an honest conversation with my in-laws and let them in on how tired and frustrated I was and ask them to help while they were visiting with us. This would include helping more around the house and taking care of the girls.*
- *Two, rather than "reacting" to not receiving help, I could have planned to get the help I wanted. I could have called a neigh-bor to help clear our driveway and walks. I could have called my mother-in-law midway through the day to ask if she could prepare the kitchen for dinner. I know she would have loved to bathe the girls and get them ready for bed, if only I'd asked. She often offered to help, and I always "batted" her help away. Because I believed I was "the only one" who could do all these things.*

When our energy feels off, it's often because we aren't being honest with ourselves and others. We stuff down our feelings, choke on our words, and get angrier than ever. If I'd been honest with my in-laws, they'd likely have risen to the occasion. And, in all fairness, if they'd excelled at giving feedback, they might have told me that they wanted to help more, but that I was making it very difficult. I hurt their feelings by not giving them feedback. And they made it worse by not speaking their truth to me. Keeping our thoughts to ourselves was not helpful to anyone.

Our energy has an impact on others. We know it. We can clear a room with our negative energy. And if we're in a leadership position at work, this hostile stress response can cause everyone around us to walk on eggshells. The result: employees won't take creative risks, won't give themselves fully to a task, and will often end up doing the bare minimum to avoid the wrath of their boss—who, as it happens, might just be you. My mother-in-law was so affected by my tense and resentful energy, she didn't know how to give me the help I needed.

I know that if I dial into a calmer, more compassionate source of energy, I draw people into the room, cultivate connection, and put people at ease. And yes, from this place I can even ask for help and receive it. If you learn to increasingly shift your energy from the stressful and angry zone to the relaxed and peaceful zone, you will find for yourself speaking from that place produces more connection, more cooperation, and better results in your every interaction. Bottom line: More often than not, you'll get the results you want.

Aligning Energy with Intention

Does that mean that a person must perpetually be in the calm and centered or "green zone" to be equipped to give feedback? No. Sometimes we genuinely feel let down and mad; however, you do have the responsibility for how you choose to "show up" when you give feedback.

Energetic alignment is a key aspect of feedback. I've talked about how aggrieved energy can create more issues than it resolves. But hey, sometimes it is appropriate to be angry or frustrated. The trick here is not to judge the energy state you are in. We get ourselves into a mess when we say words like "I'm fine" or "It's okay" when we or the situation is not okay. We think we're masking our real feelings, but our energy tells on us. It's as if our whole body is contradicting what we are saying. Our words and energy don't match. One of the biggest threats to effective feedback is the disconnect between what we are saying, or are not saying, and what is being communicated nonverbally. If you're saying one thing and energetically beaming a different message, feedback is going to fall worse than flat. So let me say this: While we desire to feel present, connected, calm, and compassionate, it's important to own our more problematic energy when it comes up and be honest about it before we move into a more neutral state. The key is to honor exactly what's going on with you.

If you are angry at a colleague or a team member because they are forever looking for excuses to have others pick up their slack, it's okay to say, "I'm frustrated with you for not completing work you committed to doing. What's going on?" Your anger isn't an excuse to go ballistic, but rather to speak from a place of honesty about how it feels to be constantly let down. But here's the thing, to control a sense of rage, you must first connect it with the fact that this is what you are feeling. If you're unaware that you're angry, your feedback may come across as aggressive or even threatening, whatever your words. But if you can acknowledge you're irate or disappointed, if you can own your emotions first, then you don't have to let them run the show. There is tremendous power in this depth of honesty. And once you tap into it by feeling the sensations in your body and identifying what you are feeling, you can say what you need to say in the way you want to say it. You're in charge.

On the other hand, there are times when we are so excited about an outcome, we feel so much joy and gratitude, we end up impulsively oversharing, overpraising, or overpromising. And when we return to a sense of reality, we may come to regret our enthusiastic praise. At that point, it's almost impossible to take back our words without creating ill will. All to say, it's important to check in with our energy, wherever it falls on the spectrum. If we know we're in an expansive mood, we can also be aware that this will affect the type of feedback we provide.

What I hope you're getting is that feedback is an art that begins by learning and exploring your own energy state. What are you experiencing? The first step is always to check in with your energy and body wisdom. There isn't anything to change initially; just be curious about what you notice about your inner thoughts, words, and body sensations, paying mind particularly to any points of tension. Once you notice your energy, the next step is to ask yourself, "Do I want to own this energy? Is it going to work for me? Or do I want to shift it?" The choice you make is about leveraging the energy that best serves your desired outcome. When you align your energy with the outcome you desire, things ebb and flow effortlessly. You find yourself being authentic, compassionate, and curious. You are more likely to make decisions based on your core beliefs, values, and insights.

Being deeply honest is to be willing to be vulnerable. It's about letting go of caring what other people think and instead giving yourself permission to say what you truly think and feel. This is how you build trust and connection. Your openness and truthfulness are key to you becoming an expert in feedback that's both compassionate and effective.

Erratic Energy Creates Fear and Uncertainty

Years ago, I had a boss who showed two different sides. Some days he would come to the office whistling, saying hello to everyone, complimenting the work of his team, treating people under stress with compassion. Then, like that, he would appear one morning meaner than a bear that just got tangled up with a hornet's nest; anger sparking from his eyes, his face set grimly, spitting out insults at the quality of everyone's work. One time I asked him if everything was okay and he reeled back, his face red, and said, "What are you talking about? Everything is FINE!" A perfect example of energetic misalignment.

It was like working for Dr. Jekyll and Mr. Hyde. Completely unpredictable. We saw deep shadows and bright lights from the same human. Several people, me among them, started looking for other jobs. Given what felt like erratic behavior, it didn't feel safe to provide this boss with feedback. What we did do, however, was ask a few of the boss's peers and his boss for some coaching to see how we could navigate these different personas and this difficult experience. We knew that others had seen the two sides and we wanted to know how to manage them better. Through our inquiry, I'm happy to say that my boss was given an opportunity by his boss to work with an executive coach. Over several months, the team started to feel a shift toward a more balanced person. We gained a boss who was able to manage himself and his emotions in a more professional manner.

While this story offers an extreme example of swinging from one end of the energy spectrum to the other, you may find yourself wondering if you don't sometimes do the same. We are only human after all, and, as I've said, our emotions are fluid. But if you tend to swing back and forth, it may be especially important to check in with yourself before a challenging conversation. If you find you are energetically down or "in the shadows" or not in a good place, see how you can shift your mood before offering feedback to another or putting yourself in the place of receiving it. As I previously mentioned, offering feedback from a place of stress isn't likely to bring about the results you desire. But nor will others be able to get through to you if you are swinging out there with your emotions in a chaotic way.

The moral of the story? Get clear on what you are feeling. Be honest with yourself and others. Don't let your shadow energy—the unclaimed and unnamed energy—take over the conversation,

Energy and Breath

"Take a deep breath." Those words, no matter who they come from, have been a negative trigger of mine for much of my life. When I hear those words, my reactive energy may push people away so that whether I say it or not, the message is the same: "Don't tell me what to do."

Recently, in studying the importance of breath as it relates to brain function, I have come to understand that to "take a deep breath" will physiologically help to get oxygen into the bloodstream, ultimately to your beating heart and your brain. Taking a breath (or several) is the only thing, *the only thing*, that makes it possible to become present to the moment, which then calms you, grounds you, brings you back to your body alignment. So, from me to you: "Take a breath."

Learning to de-stress starts with your breath. As you've already learned, if you feel stress, the feedback you provide will carry a stressful energy. The result? It won't be heard or received in a useful or meaningful way. Worse still, it can result in unintended consequences, some of them truly regrettable, such as a good worker quitting, or a valuable colleague disengaging. Which is why it's wise to take a few deep breaths and shift to doing something neutral like drinking a glass of water, looking out the window, taking a walk, or even washing your hands. Breathing and doing something that is calming will interrupt the stressful energy and create the ability for you to step back from the moment and observe the situation differently.

To notice and name what is energetically going on inside of you, you must slow down. That's the beauty of taking that breath. But you'll also want to do a body scan, to notice the signals and where you are holding tension (head, jaw, neck, shoulders, stomach, hands). Can you feel your body temperature rising? If so, take five to ten slow, deep breaths. Now, check in. Do you feel relaxed, calm, clear, cool, and connected? Or do you need to take a few more breaths or a brisk walk? The more you practice doing these simple things, the more you will learn how clean energy can fuel fantastically successful feedback.

Own It to Disarm It

One of the key practices in disarming negative energy is to own it, name it, and tell the other person what you're feeling. As an example, "You may feel my stress, or you likely sense my anger." Calmly naming what is going on for you enables the other person to understand where you are coming from and to validate their own experience of the energy you are emitting. Now, you can say, "So from this place, let me share what's going on." When you own, name, and share your energetic state, you can consciously shift from the stressed state and be responsible for how you respond, rather than unconsciously taking the stress out on another.

What I learned from the experience with my family and the simple nature of soaking my hands in warm, soapy water to wash dishes is the importance of consciously creating a neutral zone between what triggers me and how I want to respond. Selecting something that takes the attention off the trigger or stressed state—like taking a walk, listening to music, or even watching silly animal videos—creates the possibility of shifting to a more creative and relational response.

The point I am making with all of this is that many of us go through the day without consciously considering not only how we feel but also how we influence and impact others through our emotional energy. Have you ever heard the phrase "Actions speak louder than words"? Well, energy speaks louder than words too. Our energy, whether we like it or not, is constantly offering others feedback. In fact, it's like a radio station that's on 24/7, constantly transmitting background noise.

I want to stop here and return to what happened to my client who followed the Principle of Least Effort, and whose story begins this chapter. As you will recall, after his anger diffused, it was as if he had the air knocked out of him. He appeared to have no will to engage with the other person. Over time, as I worked with this client, he was able to shift from feeling deflated and avoidant to becoming confident and aware. How did this happen? Simply by taking him through the process I've just outlined: breathing to shift the flow, owning and naming his true feelings, and slowing down to take an energy scan of his body. As he connected with himself, he became clearer about what he needed to say to his co-worker. This self-awareness gave him the courage to speak his truth and tackle the situation head-on. After several conversations between my client and his peer, they found understanding, common ground, and now enjoy a collaborative and healthy conflict-based relationship.

When our energy is out of congruence with our words, the world around us feels the difference. When we are being "real" in the world around us, it means that our internal energy and our external expression are a match—we're in alignment and experience an ease with our interactions. Here's another personal story with the purpose to share an example of what I've been describing.

———————————————

When I was in my early twenties, I worked for Lee, a wonderful woman almost twenty years my senior. I loved my work and my boss, who was an amazing mentor in multiple areas of my life. She taught me many valuable lessons about who and how to be in the professional world, and how to find joy and have fun.

One day, I arrived at work in a terrible mood. While sitting at my desk that morning, Lee asked me what was wrong. I told her, "Nothing." She said, "I can tell something isn't right. Want to talk?" I snapped, "I said, Nothing! I'll be fine." Lee said, "Okay. I'm here if you need anything," and walked away.

Later that day, after our regular team meeting, she came back and gave me very specific feedback. "I don't know if you know this but your energy and whatever is going on for you today is negatively impacting and distracting the rest of the team. I think you should go take a walk around the block, shake off what is going on for you, and come back. How does that sound?"

Honestly, in the moment, I didn't think it sounded like a good idea and was quite put off by her suggestion. My initial reaction was, "Nope. I'm good. I'll stay right here and try to shake it off." Lee looked at me for a long, uncomfortable minute. I was the first one to shift. "Fine. I'll do it" was my retort. What I was thinking though was, "Why not?

It couldn't hurt to try." I knew I wasn't feeling good about what was going on inside of my mind or body.

I took a walk around the block as suggested. At first, I was wound up and angry. And then, I started to pay attention to the trees, grass, and air around me and honestly felt a little better. Not completely myself, but better. I went back to work, thanked Lee, and quietly completed my day.

The next morning as I was reading the newspaper, I came across a comic strip, which I cut out, took to work, and shared with Lee. In the first frame of the comic strip, a young girl walks up to her friend and cheerfully says, "Hi!" Her friend, a young boy, responds, "Hmph" with an angry frown on his face.

The second frame shows the girl saying in bold letters, "Oh, YOU'RE real pleasant this morning. What's the matter with you?" The response from the boy is a grumpy "Go step in front of a cement mixer, okay?" as he turns away from her.

The third frame shows the young girl screaming at her friend's back, "What a pill you are! What a jerk! Well, who needs you!? You can just stand there and be grumpy all by yourself!!"

The cartoon concludes in the fourth frame with the young girl with an angry frown on her face with "Hmph" above her head. Her friend, on the other hand, has an evil smile on his face with this thought, "Nothing helps a bad mood like spreading it around."

Ta-da! Energy transferred. Mission accomplished.

Lee laughed in delight at the comic strip and said, "How appropriate!" She then asked, "How are you feeling today?" I told her that I felt better and was grateful that she let me know how my previous day's energy had impacted others.

THOUGHTS ON FEEDBACK

Every Action in the Universe Uses Energy

According to DK Learning, an award-winning publisher, there are many types of energy such as light, heat, or movement. Energy cannot be made or destroyed. It can be stored or transferred from one object to another.

Although I secretly already knew my negative energy impacted others, it was good to have someone hold me accountable for it. Just as importantly, Lee gave me extremely specific feedback that was timely (she didn't wait until later to speak up). She illuminated how I was impacting the team, recapped the situation, and explained my specific behavior. From there she explored with me how I would respond in the future when not in a good place. It had such an impact, I still (obviously) think about that experience today.

Energy Feedback in a Virtual World

With the onset of Covid, many companies were propelled into a new virtual working world. Team meetings have been adapted and are hosted over video technology. We experience one another through little boxes on Zoom screens. Many participants choose to remain off camera, making it difficult to gather nonverbal feedback. And this situation isn't going away. Absent the visual and energetic cues we are accustomed to, it can feel as if we are operating blind. Are people listening? Are they getting the message? Are they interested? Engaged? What do they think? Speaking out on a video call can feel awkward because you're "on camera" and if the call is being recorded, your words are captured in perpetuity. How do you interrupt to ask a question when you are camera shy? This is our new world. Even when we are now able to meet in person, the prevalence of video communications has changed how the world and people communicate. Operating in a hybrid world means it's essential to be more deliberate and intentional in paying attention to energetic cues. Especially as leaders.

This may mean stepping out of your comfort zone by asking for or sharing input or feedback. This is particularly true when meeting with several people on a virtual call. The technology has been and will continue to be helpful in assisting a connected world, but if people show up to a meeting with their camera turned off, unwilling to share, it can create a sense of separation, shutout, or shutdown that threatens relationship building and team cohesion. The sense of "team connection" could be lost.

I recently attended an all-employee meeting on Zoom where the CEO and others shared important company updates. About 40 percent of the participants had their cameras on. After making an important announcement, the CEO paused, asked for feedback, and there was silence. No questions. No nods or eye contact. No visual clues with the cameras turned off. The leaders were left in the dark, both literally and metaphorically.

I believe the virtual workspace places an increased and urgent demand for bosses to communicate more if company cohesion is going to thrive. Even when you could see your employees every day in person, feedback and communication were important. Now, with miles between us, it's more essential than ever. At the same time, information devoid of connection can prove a trap. If you don't know how your communications are being received, if you can't read the energy of the room, because you aren't together in a room anymore, you can accidentally trigger all kinds of emotions that you aren't even aware of. Put bluntly, your communications could make things worse, when what you want is to make things clearer or better. So, what to do?

First and foremost, you need to find ways to check in with people. Don't just send out a company-wide communication, without asking how it landed. Don't announce a big change in policy over Zoom, without following up. If you are no longer able to read the energy of your employees because you have less contact with them, be intentional about reaching out and getting the measure of things. It's important to be more direct. Ask for feedback and share that you intend to provide more direct feedback. Without the visual and energetic cues, you may make a lot of assumptions. Clear communications create stronger connections. And, by the way, staying connected isn't just good business sense; it's important for our mental health too. If you make an extra effort to stay in two-way communication with your employees, company morale and employee well-being will be that much better.

Another simple but effective way to stay connected to people both intellectually and energetically is to make time at meetings to bring everyone into the circle. Don't be afraid to have fun. Icebreaking games, simple statements of gratitude, or an invitation to share something more personal you'd like others to know—your baby's first tooth just came in, your mother is in the hospital, your partner just got promoted—these are all important ways of creating cohesion and harmonizing energy at the group level. Sometimes it's as simple as saying, "Look, folks, I know how busy we've all been. How about we start today's meeting by taking a few deep breaths? Or a few minutes of chair-stretching?"

I've learned from experience that having some kind of ritual way of starting a meeting shifts the tone of the meeting. Don't make it arduous, long, or complicated. In today's world, more than ever, a leader must be responsible for creating team meetings that begin in intentional, meaningful, and uplifting ways.

If your team is further along and more open to sharing, you could use the energy spectrum that I illustrated earlier in the chapter. A leader I work with consistently checks in with her team this way, asking where on the energy scale they are at the start of each meeting. She told me that the value in doing this is to "set the stage" and get into her team members' worlds, acknowledging that everyone comes to each meeting a little differently. The gift of this practice is to acknowledge that we all enter meetings coming from different environments. Some are calm while some are stressful. If anything, it normalizes and acknowledges that we run the gamut of energy and emotions from moment to moment, day to day. By asking her team members where they are energetically helps my client to understand who is feeling creative, inspired, or perhaps depleted—that day. This understanding helps the entire team support one another in a non-judgmental way. And it helps the boss to understand where to insert new and different energy if needed.

If you, as a leader, are not comfortable with the examples of check-ins as I've suggested, you may want to slow down and "fine-tune" your senses. You can do this by learning to name what you notice about your own energy more freely. You can practice noticing others' energy and naming what you see. You may be surprised by how this practice makes new connections and opens us up to more meaningful communication and informative feedback.

Awakening to Energy and Feedback

I've created some statements that may help in opening this "door" around noticing energy. These aren't designed only for those working remotely. They can be used freely in all walks of life. Energy is around us all the time. The way we interact with one another. What we sense from each other. And what we give off. When we slow down just enough, we can notice what we are feeling, what the experience is, and then name it.

A few months ago, I walked into a client's office to meet one-on-one with her. I had known this client for approximately a year. I immediately noticed a tense energy and my client felt "prickly." As I put my computer on the desk, I asked, "Hey there. Is everything okay? The energy here feels a little off today."

The response I received was abrupt. The person jumped up and exclaimed very loudly, "What? Why would you say that? I don't appreciate your judging me. This meeting is over. I'm not talking with you right now. How dare you judge me!"

I didn't expect that response. I picked up my belongings and said, "I'm sorry you feel this way. I didn't mean to insinuate anything. Let me know when/if you want to meet with me today. You know where to find me."

As I walked out of her office, I was blown away by her reaction and at the same time was curious about what had set her off. My intuition about energy had been right. It wasn't just prickly; it was explosive. My last thought as I went back to working on a project was, "I hope she's okay."

A few hours later, this client came by the office where I was working. My face softened as I looked up, anticipating an apology for her outburst. I didn't get that. What I got was, "I really don't appreciate your judging me all of the time and want to ask you to stop."

I said, "I'm confused. I was noticing the energy in the room and asked if you were okay. I'm sorry if my comment made you feel judged."

Again, she exploded, "Stop it! Stop judging me." And stormed off.

I spoke about the incident with my coach later that day as I wanted to try to figure out what I might have done so I could sort through how to or if to approach the topic again. My coach reminded me that I am just one part of the equation in that relationship and suggested that I wait a few days to reapproach that person. Which I did.

A few days after the original "incident" I stopped by my client's office and said, "I haven't been feeling good about the situation from a few days ago. Is there anything you can tell me that will help me understand what happened? Specifically, what of my behaviors made you feel judged? I value you. I'm curious and interested in the feedback."

The client said, "What you are doing right now by asking these questions makes me feel like I'm under a microscope and that you are dissecting and judging me. Please stop. Just work on and deliver your projects."

"All right. I hear you loud and clear" was all I could say at the time. I turned around and left her office.

For the remainder of the contract, I kept that relationship at arm's length, speaking only about project progress, deliverables, and implementation.

But as I reflect on this story, I also realize that it's no wonder we humans can become over-sensitized and suffer from inner voices that stop us from giving feedback. I had triggered something in this person. And her reaction also shut me down. And it's unfortunate. But the truth is, if you keep waiting for the right time for someone to be open or receptive about receiving feedback, it's not going to happen. People may get defensive when they receive feedback. It just happens. Don't let what they are going to do get in the way of what you must do. If you care about someone enough, you'll give them the feedback they need and trust that they will respond as they will from their lens, their truth. It's not your job to manage how they receive the feedback. It's your job to manage how you provide feedback. And as illustrated in the case above, how you receive their feedback. For me, in the above situation, I respected her perspective. I chose to listen to her request to back off, buckle down, and keep quiet.

While invisible, so much about our ability to connect with and the way we relate to the world around us is about energy. Oftentimes, we can't put a finger on or articulate what is going on, but we sense something is off or "prickly." This happens when we can't seem to connect with someone or when someone always annoys us. It's often hard to really say why, and yet it impacts our relationships and productivity.

Making a practice of noticing and naming energy, even if you don't get it quite right, will create new and meaningful relationships.

Statements like, "I'm noticing that I'm feeling a bit resistant to this idea. Can I process it before I commit?"

Or "My mind is exploding with ideas. I'm excited to explore this idea a little more. What about you? What are you feeling?"

Or "I have the energy to do this project—do you?"

Naming your energy is often the first step for truth-telling. The energy around something is going to come out anyway, whether consciously or not. For example, if someone is resistant about working on a project, but not saying it, it's going to show up anyway. It will show up in missed deadlines or incomplete work. Wouldn't it be better if verbal feedback like "I'm resistant to working on this project" were provided? This way, a collaborative effort could be made to work through the resistance.

Conversely, if someone is excited about a project, you'll feel enthusiasm, see the results, and often find that work is turned in on time if not early.

There are many avenues to explore the nature of energy by noticing it daily. Energy shows up in so many ways. If you incorporate some of the following keywords into noticing what's going on for you, it may open opportunities for others in your life to follow suit.

- Excitement, joyful (high vibration)
- Creative, innovative
- Loving

- Annoyance, impatience, restlessness
- Tension, walking on eggshells
- Angry (red zone)
- Dismissive (like someone has turned their back)
- Protective (arms crossed, body energy closed off)
- Overwhelming or overwhelmed
- Resistant
- Shut down

The energy of feedback shows up in places you would never think about. And when you are fully conscious about connecting with energy, you'll find it—all around you and everywhere.

Practicing Mastery in Energy

In addition to what you've gained in this chapter, you have an opportunity to practice mastery in energy using these other examples of where our energy can influence how we show up and have impact on how we may provide feedback:

- Tired
- Sick
- Out of sorts
- Stressed
- Angry
- Excited
- Calm
- Joyful
- Love

If you aren't familiar with the nature of your energy, I would encourage you to practice noticing it for five minutes each day. Consider taking a moment to explore what your body is telling you. It's likely that your "thinking" brain is dominant, which is why it's important to access your body. Listen to your body and its cues on where you feel happy, excited, tense, resistant, tired, or other things. What are your neck, shoulders, back, heart, stomach, hands, hips, feet, and other parts of your body telling you?

REFLECTIONS / PRACTICES

Think about and write a few examples of situations where you are "taking in" or observing interpersonal energy. *An example could be, "Her face was red, and I could sense her anger even though she said she wasn't angry." Or "When I'm around him, I feel so alive! He has an invisible infectious cheerfulness."*

Think about situations and write a few examples of when you are "giving out" Interpersonal Energy. *An example could be when someone says to you, "Are you okay? You seem really frustrated." Or "There's something about you. You seem 'lighter' today."*

Bonus:

At the end of each day for 30 days, reflect by writing in your journal or on your calendar areas where you noticed Interpersonal Energy "showing up" in your life. What have you experienced with other people and/or what have you noticed about yourself?

Extra Bonus (a gift from the Stress Reset™)

When you feel like you are in the stress response or red zone as described earlier in this chapter, I invite you to follow these steps:

Step 1: Stop. You are not in actual danger.

Step 2: Breathe. Take 5-10 deep, slow, cleansing breaths.

Step 3: Do something that makes you feel good or grounds you.

Take a walk. Listen to music. Play with an animal. Call a friend.This is considered the relaxation response or green zone.

Step 4: Check in. What is your energy now? Do you need to repeat Steps 2 and 3 or are you good to proceed?

KEY TAKEAWAY

Part of giving and receiving feedback is having awareness to the nonverbal messaging that you receive internally (via emotions and physiological responses) and exude externally (via body language, facial cues, etc.). Bringing awareness to your energy state informs you of feedback given without saying a word.

CHAPTER 5

Creating the Optimal Environment for Feedback

Out beyond ideas of wrongdoing and rightdoing,
there is a field. I'll meet you there.

~Rumi

I was visiting a client site and meeting with a few employees in a conference room with the door open. During our meeting we overheard a loud, angry voice say, "I'm sick of having this information turned in inaccurately! Forget it. I'll just have to do it myself. Get out of here and pull the door closed behind you when you leave."

We heard the door close. And then a deep muffled voice walked by the conference room saying, "I can't get anything right. I might as well quit."

The scenario described above is one I have experienced far too many times. It's when feedback is given at the wrong time and the wrong place. In this case, other employees and an outside consultant overheard the exchange, causing general upset and embarrassment. I'd like to say this was an outlier, but in truth most people blurt out feedback without thinking about the appropriate environment in which it should take place. So in the chapter ahead, I want to share what I've learned about the best environments for giving feedback, gathered from my wide variety of exposure to workplace culture and effectiveness over many years. We'll be considering both internal (self) and external (physical) environments. And while there is no perfect environment, I have learned that there are specific conditions that apply in almost all situations when giving impactful feedback.

Internal Environment

Our internal environment is about what's going on inside of us and takes into consideration our thoughts and belief systems. This includes the way we see ourselves and others and how we make sense of the world around us. How we view our own strengths and weaknesses compared to others can impact our thoughts. Our self-worth and self-regard are also part of what constitutes our belief systems. So does how we process and provide information and what triggers us. These internal beliefs and operating systems are key drivers in what influence our external behaviors, such as how we communicate and the energy we emit. Our internal environment or beliefs generate "self-talk," which creates feelings, producing reactions and behaviors related to an event.

Consider the range of internal belief systems that exist. For example, on one end as described in Figure 5, you may feel as though you must control everything and do everything yourself. On the other end, you may trust that everything is going to turn out just as it's supposed to and that there are people who can help you to achieve that. And then there is everything in between. These belief systems guide our thoughts and ultimately our behaviors, actions, and communication in everything we do. Including giving feedback.

Controlling Must do everything Must be number one	Everything in between	Connecting Others will help We all win

FIGURE 5

When our internal belief system is that we must control and do everything ourselves, our communications are likely to be expressed as criticism, judgment, or resentment. Very few employees will meet our high standards, if we believe we're the only ones who know how to get things done. I've heard the following from leaders when they are in the controlling belief state: "Idiots. Why can't they just do it right the first time?" Or "I guess I have to take over the work and do it myself to get this done correctly!" In this frame of mind, a leader is unlikely to offer feedback to the employee whom they perceive is in the wrong. This, of course, results in the inability of the employee to get it right the next time. With no patience to train or develop the person they are criticizing, the leader will complain to anyone who will listen that they've hired a bunch of "morons" who can't do their jobs right. This kind of leader is a perfect example of someone who is fueled by a belief system that "they have to do everything," which eventually leads to resentment and righteousness.

But what if our internal belief system operates from a place of connection? In this scenario, a leader will likely reach out to others to talk about what needs to be done, invite ideas, and ask for help. I've seen this type of leader say to someone, "This request just came from our Board of Directors. It needs to be completed within the week, and I could use some assistance. I know that you have the background and experience in this area. Are you willing to help, and can you meet this deadline?" The employee agrees to help. As the week ends, the leader who made the request notices that the deliverable isn't as expected. The leader goes back to the employee and says, "What you gave me isn't exactly what we discussed and agreed to. The adjustment I need to see made is ____. Can you do that by the end of the day? What other support or assistance do you need from me or someone on the team to make this happen?"

See? Two different types of internal systems (or environments) resulting in two remarkably different behaviors. In the end, the outcome may be the same. But in the first case, everything depends on the leader. If they get sick, if they can't do it all, then real problems arise, because there's no one to pick up the slack. In the second scenario, there are simply more hands on deck, and everyone knows what needs to happen to make something occur. If the leader needs to focus their attention elsewhere, the teams can still get results. And, let's face it, which organization would you rather be a part of? The one in which you are empowered, or the one in which you are told you keep getting it wrong?

The graph, of course, has a large section called "Everything in between." I want to say a few words about this too. There are times when taking total control can work and may even be necessary. But the more you can practice the internal belief system of connection, the more you will build a robust, responsive, and resilient workplace. If at first you find yourself somewhere in the middle, that between place, it's fine. Notice what works. How you feel when you act from a more connected perspective. How the people around you respond. Notice how your ability to communicate clearly and give constructive feedback can help others to help you. As you do this, you will naturally find yourself moving into Connection.

Coming at Feedback from a Good Place

Most particularly for those who fall more into the controlling belief system, feedback poses another challenge. The truth is none of us have complete control over how a person on the other end of our feedback will receive it. For some, feedback reads as criticism. And criticism is apt to evoke all kinds of neurological responses such as fear, flight, or fight. These are all generated from our amygdala, which looks like an almond-shaped mass of gray matter inside each cerebral hemisphere. While small, the amygdala has a big job determining how emotions are experienced. It is there to warn us of any threat that comes our way.

The reason I am spending time with the amygdala is to introduce the power of the neurological aspects that occur within us, even without being fully conscious and present to what is driving our fears. The amygdala's job is to scan the environment with the intent of keeping us out of danger. It is therefore a primary driver in the "how" of feedback.

For feedback to be both given and received in such a way that it is impactful and meaningful, three essential aspects need to be present.

Internal State in Giving Feedback

We all operate from our internal state regardless of whether it occurs consciously or unconsciously. At any given time of day, our internal state of being can shift. Depending on what that state is, it will affect the way we think, feel, and act.

To better explain, I will use a reference from the book *The 15 Commitments of Conscious Leadership*. The authors (Jim Dethmer, Diana Chapman, and Kaley Warner Klemp) created what they believe is the most important model for a conscious leader. That is, are you operating from above the line or below the line?

Above the line, we are open, curious, and committed to learning. Below the line, we are closed, defensive, and committed to being right. When thinking occurs from below the line, it's often the amygdala in the driver's seat (danger, danger). This response may be triggered by a previous traumatic or upsetting experience. It's as if we barely know what's happened before we snap at someone or say something we'll only regret later. So, a great question to ask yourself prior to providing feedback is this: "Am I above or below the line?"

I frequently use this model in coaching my clients, especially when they are preparing to give key feedback or to receive it. These tools let them easily identify their internal state of mind. Regardless of what that is, we spend time exploring what they are feeling and thinking, who they want to be, and how they want to offer their gift of feedback.

The following story is an illustration of how our internal state affects how we offer feedback, and how we can shift from "below the line" to "above the line."

Sarah had offered a free six-month training program to a group of women. After the training program ended, one particular woman would frequently contact Sarah wanting advice, coaching, resources, and ideas about networking. She would also ask for time to meet via Zoom, and Sarah would respond promptly with several possible dates and times. Then Sarah would hear nothing, for weeks on end. Then, out of the blue, the woman would email again with several reasons why she couldn't or hadn't responded to Sarah in a timely manner, meanwhile asking, "Are you free NOW?"

While Sarah was giving the backstory, she became noticeably agitated. Sarah said, "It would be one thing if it were an occasional situation. But it happens ALL the time. After she contacts me, I respond, and then she disappears on me. I feel resentful. Taken advantage of. Disrespected. Triggered. I want to punish her because I feel I've been treated badly. I think about all the responses I am going to email her with:

...Do you realize you ALWAYS do this?

...I've reached out to you; you never get back to me.

...Do you realize how incredibly annoying you are?
...Why do you think it's okay to waste my precious time?
...You're constantly wasting my time.
...I feel taken advantage of."

Sarah continued, "Because my responses feel reactive and punishing, I find that I do nothing, because I'm sure I'll say something I will regret later. Which, of course, doesn't change the situation."

As we talked, Sarah noticed her own triggers in the situation. Her own internal chatter. The stories she was making up.

One recycled story that Sarah came up with was, "I don't matter as much as you do." Or "I'm not as important as you are."

Sarah went on to say, "What I know about myself is that when I bring my old story into the present, rather than giving really honest feedback, I become defensive and punitive."

We talked about what it would look like if Sarah turned the lens around. As we did this, she realized that the first steps would be the same as before but look different:

1. Notice the trigger. (Stop, notice)
2. What am I making the trigger mean? (Story, curiosity)
3. How do I want to be with this person? (Relationship, connection)
4. What is the optimal outcome I'd like to see?

Sarah said, "What I really want to do with this woman is to point out the cost of her behavior and the negative impact it has had on me, and in a way that does not make her out to be a bad person."

Sarah went on to say, "What I want for myself, and my own internal state and sense of freedom is to let go of the feeling of resentment that I have for this woman. While I don't feel entirely grateful to her or for her, I want to feel empowered to express what is there for me that helps her move on."

I asked, "What kind of relationship do you want to have with her?"

Sarah contemplated this question. "Really? I think I'm done with her.

I've given her all that I want to give her and it's time for her to move on."

I said, "That says a lot, Sarah. So, what feedback do you want to give her?"

Sarah lit up. "Oh, that's the shift. Yes. I would respond this way: [Name of woman], you have everything you need to do this work in your own beautiful and particular way. You absolutely have my permission to use my work if you reference the source. Given all you've learned, I know you'll do a wonderful job. I wish you the best."

Sarah was thoughtful, and her face softened as she noticed her own internal shift. "I would be moving from being angry with her (for the inconvenience) to supporting her and wishing her well. By doing this, I am providing honest feedback and closure for her. And for me, as well. What's more, I won't have to feel any regret or guilt for speaking out of anger or resentment."

Sarah's story illustrates how complex giving feedback can be. There are so many things happening behind the scenes that we're unaware of and that are rooted in our "stories." But by slowing down and paying attention to our internal state, we can give genuine rather than reactive feedback. As mentioned earlier in the chapter, your brain catalogs vast amounts of information and drives your experiences, and especially your stories. Your "stories" are those unconscious thoughts that run in the background of your life. They are influenced by your past and are always happy to jump into any situation that presents itself. For each of us, our stories are different. What doesn't change is that our stories reflect how we see and experience the world. So, if your story or internal belief system is that everyone is out to get you because someone once hurt you, then that's the lens through which you'll see the world. And if your story is that people want to do a good job, because that's what you've experienced in the past, then that will affect how you relate to your peers and employees. But the past is rarely a perfect predictor of the future, and who wants to get trapped in a cycle of seeing every situation based on an internal bias?

Take, for example, a recent conversation with a friend of mine where we talked about getting together. When I suggested meeting later that very day, he said, "You know, I'm tired. Can we meet another time?"

My external response was, "Sure, that would be great. Let me know what would work for you."

Internally, however, I noticed the voice in my head that chimed in, "Sure. Sure thing. You're always tired. I bet we'll never get together." Granted, my immediate judgment was based on a few past experiences. But not on The Truth. That's how fast stories show up (Figure 6).

Stories Come From

Past experiences
Assumptions
Opinions
Beliefs
Judgments
Interpretations
Perceptions

FIGURE 6

Let's look more closely at how stories impact our ability to provide feedback.

A few years ago, a client of mine and I were talking about an employee who wasn't performing as expected. As we discussed the situation, my client said, "I would love to see the employee's performance improve, but I can't say anything. The last two times I brought up this issue, my employee got defensive, completely shut down, and avoided me for a few days. I'd rather not say anything."

My internal alarm bells were ringing loudly and an inner voice said, "What?! Hold up here."

"Okay, so let me get this straight," I said. "You have an employee that isn't performing. The purpose of giving feedback is to help the employee develop and perform. And you're choosing not to because you have a story that the employee will get defensive, shut down, and avoid you. Is this right?"

"Yes. Sounds a little crazy when you say it, but yes. I'm afraid that the employee will shut down again."

Ah, yes. That's it. Fear gets in the way when we let our past experiences or stories drive our decisions. Good old fear.

"It's not crazy," I said, but it's not going to get you or the employee the results you are looking for. Not saying anything isn't going to help your employee grow, right? Let's try it a different way. Tell me about the employee. What does she bring to you, the team, and the organization?"

My client thought and said, "I value this employee so much. She's smart, analytical, collaborative. She sees the big picture and connections in ways that the rest of the team doesn't. What's getting in her way is that she isn't good at checking details and is making small, but impactful mistakes. I want her to slow down, really investigate the details, and in doing so, I believe her performance will improve."

"Excellent," I said. "I hear and appreciate how much you value this employee and want her to improve. By focusing on both what you value and the purpose of why the feedback is important, I know we can get

you to the place of delivering the feedback powerfully and without fear. And, hopefully, in a manner that the employee will be able to hear."

"It's certainly worth a try."

"Have you ever told your employee what you just told me about how valuable she is?"

"I think so, though I probably didn't say to her what I just said to you because I was focused on fixing the lack of attention to details."

"What impact do you think your sharing what you see as her value, along with the purpose of the feedback, and the improvement area she needs to focus on, would have on the employee?"

My client was thoughtful. "You know, I don't know how the employee will react, but as I think about providing her with the whole picture, it may help her make the connections. It's certainly worth a try."

"If I may, would you be open to some additional context to add to your conversation?"

"Sure! Any other suggestions would be helpful."

"What if you were to start the conversation by naming your fear, story, and purpose too? Something like this: '[Employee name], you are an extremely valuable employee on our team. You're smart, analytical, collaborative. You see the big picture and connections in ways that the rest of the team doesn't. I really appreciate your contributions. There is one area of your performance that is getting in the way and is holding you back. I'd like to provide you with specific feedback; however, I'm afraid that you will get defensive again. It's happened a couple of times, which has caused me to hesitate; however, I'm doing you a disservice in your growth and development by being afraid of your reaction. I truly value you and I would love to see this one area improve so that you can continue to grow and develop in your role. Would you be willing to hear my feedback and explore this?'"

A few weeks after we met, my client called and told me that she had tried this new approach. Though she felt super vulnerable and was afraid to get it wrong, she forged ahead. She said that while the *conversation had started out a bit awkwardly, it ended up with a great outcome. She explained it was awkward because she didn't really know how to start and at one point, the employee got defensive. My client told me she was brave enough to say to her employee, "That's the defensiveness that I'm talking about." To which the employee paused and responded, "Oh. I see what you mean." The employee listened to her feedback and asked for time to process. They agreed to stop the conversation and reconvene the next day.*

When they reconnected, the employee told my client, "I get it now. I've been told that I get defensive and shut down before, but it wasn't until you took the time to lay everything out for me that I was able to see how I react. I will do my best to be open to feedback in the future. Thank you for taking the time to let me know where I am doing well and where I can do better. I am committed to improving my performance."

Here's the thing: When it's time to give feedback, we often let our fear grow bigger and more important so that it overshadows the purpose of feedback. To overcome this, I encourage you to switch things around— to amplify the purpose of offering feedback so that it overshadows the fear. But first, let's look at how the purpose of feedback shows up:

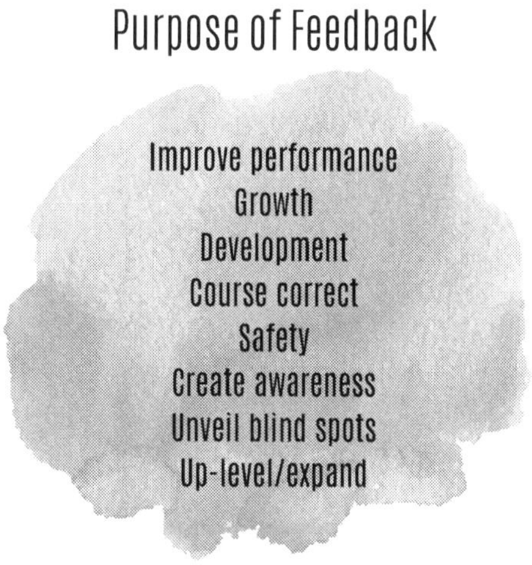

Purpose of Feedback

Improve performance
Growth
Development
Course correct
Safety
Create awareness
Unveil blind spots
Up-level/expand

FIGURE 7

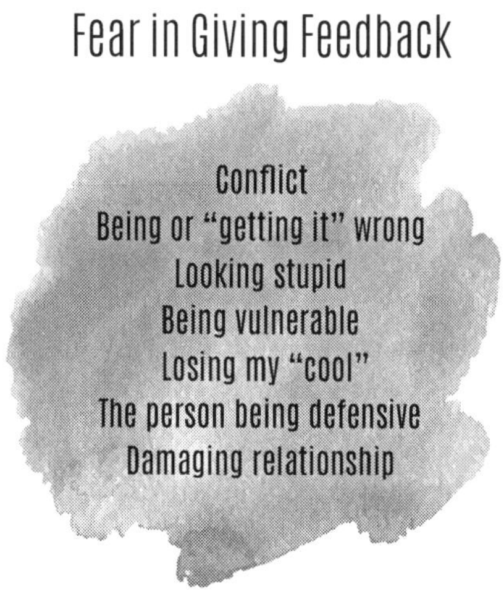

Fear in Giving Feedback

Conflict
Being or "getting it" wrong
Looking stupid
Being vulnerable
Losing my "cool"
The person being defensive
Damaging relationship

FIGURE 8

The true purpose of giving feedback (Figure 7) is about helping others see things they can't about themselves. We aren't built to see ourselves as others see us. And while sometimes uncomfortable, when someone provides us with feedback with the purpose of creating awareness, to course correct or to improve performance, and it's received as such, changes are made and growth occurs. Think about my introductory story about Marc and me. His true purpose was to help me see what everyone else (but me) could see. He invited me to see their perspective so that I could choose how I wanted to show up next.

Next time you're in the position of giving feedback, think about whether your **FEAR** is bigger than your **PURPOSE** or your **PURPOSE** is bigger than your **FEAR** (Figure 8). And choose which you want to lead with.

State of Being

One final thing I will mention prior to moving to the external environment is to consider our Internal State of Being: As mentioned earlier in the chapter, what you are bringing to the conversation will depend a lot on how it goes. Consider the following chart:

Internal State for Giving Feedback

Internal State	Existing State	Desired State
Consider how you feel	Irritable	Grateful
Inner state thinking	I hate having to do this	I'm glad I am available to do this
Inner state feeling	Resentment	Connection
Physical feeling	Clenched, tight, tired	Open, expansive, energetic
Breath	Rapid and/or holding breath	Relaxed, calm breath
Mindset	Fixed	Growth
Sensations	Overwhelmed, anxious	Calm, curious

FIGURE 9

Notice where you are starting from, internally. And then choose if and how you want to shift. If you need to, refer to the chapter that discusses energy. How do you want the conversation to go? The ball is in your court.

Creating the External Environment

The physical space in which you provide feedback matters. A noisy bar, an open-plan office with no privacy, the corridor between meeting rooms—these are not optimal places for feedback. Just as you want to create a calm and spacious internal state of mind, it helps to create a positive external environment. So just how do we go about doing that?

Physical space includes all the aesthetic elements that make up that space. Things to consider here are: Is the space private, quiet, a place where you won't be interrupted? Or would a livelier, bustling environment, like a café, feel more appropriate and less threatening? Is the space neutral to both parties? Is the noise level such that you can easily hear each other without being overheard, especially by other colleagues? I like to incorporate spaciousness into the mix. Places like the outdoors (taking a walk), open courtyards in office parks, and strolling through a museum (to provide creative flow) come to mind for me. These places feel open, expansive, and creative. Additionally, allowing sufficient time for the feedback session is important so that parties don't feel rushed.

External Environment Checklist

		Create your checklist
☐ In private	☐ In public	☐ _____
☐ In person	☐ Not in person	☐ _____
☐ Inside	☐ Text	☐ _____
☐ Sitting	☐ Phone call	☐ _____
☐ Table	☐ Zoom/Teams/GoogleMeet	☐ _____
☐ Chairs	☐ People around	☐ _____
☐ Couch	☐ No one around	☐ _____
☐ Countertop/Stools	☐ Ambient sound	☐ _____
☐ Florescent lights	☐ No sound	☐ _____
☐ Dim lights	☐ Driving	☐ _____
☐ Natural light	☐ Standing	☐ _____
☐ Outside	☐ In an office	☐ _____
☐ Walking	☐ At a coffee shop	☐ _____
☐ Where? _____	☐ Other? _____	☐ _____

FIGURE 10

In considering the external environment, I would encourage you to take a meta-view. Imagine you are a director for a Broadway production or on a movie set. How do you see having a conversation where you are able to provide feedback and it's received in the best possible way?

Perhaps the simple checklist above will help.

THOUGHTS ON FEEDBACK

What Does Our Environment Have to Do with Feedback?

People rarely think about the best external environment for providing feedback. But if you're only thinking about how and not where, you may be undermining your best efforts.

How often have you thought about the external environment when giving feedback to another? If we are honest with ourselves, we are typically too concerned about getting out what we have been bottling up inside, and don't think much about the circumstances or the environment. And yet, environment plays a key role in how we show up. Some of us feel great in quiet spaces, or out in nature. Others of us like a comfortable chair and cup of coffee in hand. Others of us prefer to offer feedback in a business-like setting, because it allows for "boundaries" and is professional. There's no right or wrong to this; it's about finding an environment that brings out your best, and doesn't overwhelm, intimidate, or distract from the person to whom you are offering feedback. The following suggestions can work in your favor, regardless of whether feedback is given in person or remotely. What is important to remember is that "setting the stage" for feedback is as important as the feedback itself. Case in point:

I was working in a predominantly male organization and industry. Our chief human resources officer (CHRO) was a woman whom I admired. She was intelligent, business-minded, professional, and able to "hold her own" with her male peers and board members. A "no-nonsense" leader, she was firm and when not in reaction mode, fair. However, for a certain period while working with her, she inexplicably adopted "Reaction" as her middle name.

I had co-facilitated a three-hour presentation to a group of general managers on a new strategic HR initiative we were rolling out. After finishing our presentation, we all took a break and while walking out, the CHRO loudly requested that my peer and I stay behind for a quick discussion. Even before everyone filed out of the conference room, she exploded, yelling at us, her face flushed and arms flailing. If I wanted to exaggerate, but only slightly, I would say she was spitting rocks.

My colleague and I were stunned. We couldn't believe what was occurring. We had collaborated on the presentation with the CHRO. We had practiced the presentation several times. We had double- and triple-checked the details and outcome of the strategy. We found out later that for a split moment before our CHRO asked us to stay behind, we both thought we had "rocked" the presentation.

During the "explosive" feedback session, we learned from the CHRO that we hadn't incorporated some final input and a date change that she had sent us an hour before our presentation. She was livid that we hadn't caught the detail in time. She then demanded what we were going to do to remedy the situation and by when.

Paralyzed by the outburst, we tripped over one another to apologize, concerned we were going to be fired. I think we also both knew at that moment that there wasn't a good answer or explanation.

When we walked out of the conference room, we passed by several general managers. None of them had any words to share, but it was *clear by their eyes—catching ours and then looking to the floor or away—they had heard the entire exchange. How embarrassing.*

The next day, my co-worker and I stepped into my boss's office and asked her if we could speak with her about the presentation. After she said yes, we quietly closed the door. I remember bravely starting the conversation. I said that we wanted to apologize for missing the last-minute changes. And we understood her frustration from the previous day, but we didn't appreciate how or where her feedback had been delivered. My co-worker went on to say we felt humiliated, embarrassed, and disrespected by her choice of such a public place. We asked her to consider giving this type of feedback in private in the future. Our boss was surprised by the request and said, "No." She didn't see her outburst as anything to be embarrassed about. She just wanted to get her point across before we wrapped up the session.

We thanked her for her time, left her office, and considered (as most would) if this was the environment and culture where we wanted to cultivate our careers.

Reflecting on what happened, I want to take us on a bit of a journey exploring the internal state and external state of the circumstance, now that we have the criteria with which to evaluate them.

Let's consider what we've learned thus far:

- My boss was likely more controlling than curious that day.
- We were all operating below the line. The exchange of and listening to information wasn't going to happen. Someone had to be right, someone had to be wrong.
- Our energy was in the stress response.
- My boss's purpose was larger than her fear in giving feedback. I would say regardless of the "environmental factors," she wanted immediate course correction.

- The external environment wasn't a thought (or was it?) for my boss. She certainly chose the public environment as the forum for feedback. And based on the follow-up conversation the next day, she was perfectly fine with her choice regardless of the impact.

Here's what I learned from that experience. I hope I never humiliate another human being in the manner that my boss humiliated my co-worker and me that day. Let me just say, she taught me a lot about "how not to give feedback."

Here's a "better story" of setting the environment for feedback:

In 2015, I attended a local Society for Human Resource Management (SHRM) Talent Management conference. It was my first conference in a couple of years, and I was excited to attend the program and network with people in the new city I moved to. Prior to attending the conference, I made myself a promise to get the most out of the conference and to provide feedback on speakers and sessions.

The keynote speaker was Ben Casnocha, an entrepreneur, author, and venture capitalist who regularly speaks about how to attract talent. I found his presentation informative, insightful, and inspiring. I had several key takeaways and I wanted him to know that he had made an impact on me. My thinking about talent attraction and management had evolved because of his talk. After Ben spoke, I immediately found my way to the front of the room and asked him if he had a few minutes. There were several other people around and yet he said, "Yes." I said, "I'd like to provide you with some feedback. Is this a good place for you or would you like to go someplace private?" Ben smiled and said, "I'm great with receiving your feedback right here."

I told him how I had found this presentation inspiring and gave specifics about the ideas I would be taking away and implementing. Ben responded by thanking me for the feedback, which reassured him *that his keynote had offered tangible value. We exchanged cards and went into our next sessions. Asking permission to provide feedback in that environment set the stage for both of us to be present. It made a small moment, in a big conference, stand out because of the quality of connection and the sharing.*

Making Sure the "Feedback" Environment Serves Your Purpose

Internal Environment:

When preparing to provide feedback, take a minimum of five minutes to sit still, reflect, and notice how you are feeling inside. Is your attitude reflective of the best possible state to provide constructive feedback? If not, what do you need to do to shift to a more conducive internal state?

Then, take time to reflect on the following questions. They invite you to consider the person you will be speaking with, the relationship you have with them, and the purpose of the feedback. Getting clear before you speak can help direct what you want to say and allow you to feel confident in the process. My advice: Whenever possible, don't offer feedback until you've answered these questions for yourself. With practice, you will do it naturally and automatically, but until then, make sure you have these questions close at hand.

- Who will you be providing feedback to?
- What is your **Relationship** with that person?
- What is your **Intention** or **Purpose** in providing the feedback?
- Do you have **Respect** for the person? If so, why? If not, why not?
- Do you have a **Growth** mindset for the **Outcome** you want to create?
- What **Connection or Relationship** do you want to have after the feedback is provided?

- Do you have **Permission** to provide the feedback?
- What is your **Commitment** in helping with the growth and development of the person you are speaking with?
- Do you notice any **Judgment** in how you are thinking about the person? If so, where is it coming from? Can you set it aside?
- What **Curiosity** can you bring to the conversation?
- What do you hope to **Learn** from the person you are giving feedback to?
- How will you **Conclude** the feedback experience?

After concluding your feedback, how will you measure its success? The questions below will help you evaluate your feedback session. It's important to note, these are not intended to have you beat up on yourself if things went less than perfectly. Remember, feedback is an art that takes practice. But awareness is the key to mastery. This is just information. It's also a powerful means of giving yourself feedback on, well, feedback!

- Did you deliver the feedback as you intended?
- What did you notice throughout the feedback conversation?
- What did you learn about the receiver?
- Did the person receive the feedback as intended? How do you know?

External Environment:

Depending on what kind of feedback you plan to offer, from rich praise to a performance assessment, the external environment might change. For example, if you want to celebrate a star employee, a public space might work beautifully. Ask yourself: What experience would you like the receiver of your feedback to walk away with when you are complete with your feedback? Remember, you have the opportunity, responsibility, and power to design the feedback session as you would like, right down to the external environment in which it is delivered. So, let's consider some different scenarios. If the intention of your feedback is to:

- **Provide praise:** What do you know about your employee? How do they prefer to receive praise? Could this feedback occur in public?
- **Provide constructive feedback (aka criticism):** What do you know about your employee? How do they like to receive constructive feedback? What type of environment would help them feel safe and be open to exploring what's next?
- **Provide performance feedback:** What do you know about your employee and how they prefer to receive performance feedback? Do you know what environment would make them the most comfortable and open? If possible, I would suggest that rather than sitting across from the employee that you sit next to or with the employee. This is a better way of indicating that "we're in this together."
- **Acknowledgment:** What do you know about your employee and how they like to be acknowledged? Could this feedback occur in a public place?

The purpose for providing these examples is to help you think about the nuances and importance of the optimal environment for feedback. The type of feedback should be part of your deliberation in choosing a space. While nothing is set in stone, it is common sense that when you have something hard or quite critical to say, it's best to say it in a controlled environment in which you will not be interrupted and where you can have privacy. If the feedback is more generally in the "good job" category, you might feel less constrained and open to more creative options. Additionally, while certain technology is convenient and important, I would encourage that authentic, meaningful feedback be provided either in person (face to face) or over a video or phone call. I would veer away from sending an IM/DM, text, or Slack message.

When providing feedback to others, don't expect (or demand) that the person responds right away. In some circumstances, extroverted types will respond immediately, while more introverted employees will prefer to wait. Many people need to process feedback before responding. For those who are introverted or are latent processors, it is valuable and considerate to ask if they need clarification, but then allow time and space to process prior to expecting a full response. You will, in these cases, want to make sure to follow up in a timely fashion.

Co-Creating the Optimal Environment for Feedback

One of the things about working with leaders is that we think we know it all when it comes to other people. My favorite statements from leaders include:

"I don't want to say it this way, because I know they'll take it that way." How do you know?

"Of course, they love to be recognized in public. Who doesn't?" How do you know?

"I don't think s/he is going to do anything with my feedback." How do you know?

One thing you can do as a leader is to stop assuming that you know how others think. Instead, find out how exactly your employees like to receive feedback. I call this "co-creating the optimal environment for feedback." You and the employee get to create what will work for both of you.

I would encourage you to "set the stage" for the feedback environment with all employees whether through the interview, onboarding, or a 1:1 meeting process by:

- Bringing to light the cultural aspects of how feedback aligns with the organization's mission, vision, and values.

- Asking the employee how s/he likes to receive feedback.
- Learning how the employee processes feedback.
- Letting the employee know that your feedback will be based on your experience, perception, observation, and expectations.
- Providing permission for the employee to be curious about and perhaps negotiate the exchange of feedback.
- Sharing with the employee how you like to receive feedback and how you process the information.
- Inviting a consistent cadence on being comfortable with giving and receiving feedback.

Here's an example of how a misstep provided the opportunity to get on the same page about how to give and receive feedback.

On a Friday afternoon, a leader called her employee and said, "I need to schedule time with you on Monday to provide you with feedback."

The employee said, "Really? You're letting me know now that you are going to provide me with feedback on Monday? What is the feedback about?"

The leader said, "This can wait until Monday."

The employee said, "I don't think it can. If the feedback were good, you would have already given it. Now I'm worried and whether you share your feedback, my weekend is already ruined by worry and stress about what you are going to say."

"Well, don't get mad at me for telling you now."

"I'm already mad. Just tell me."

The leader went on to provide feedback to the employee.

At the end of the conversation, the employee said, "Thank you for sharing this feedback. It truly really wasn't as bad as I made it out to be in my mind. Please don't do that to me again. If you need to provide me with feedback, just get on with it. Don't make me wait."

The leader and employee agreed to keep the lines of communication open for providing feedback freely and when needed.

As I've shared throughout this chapter, creating the optimal environment, both internally and externally, is invaluable to providing powerful and meaningful feedback. It also provides a more connected relationship between people. Taking the time to thoughtfully cultivate the best environments will create a connected relationship with your employee and achieve better results for you, the employee, your organization, and your customers.

REFLECTIONS / PRACTICES

- Take notice of when you feel most centered, calm, and connected (internally and externally).
- Notice your environment. Where do you see feedback being given? What do you notice about a person's internal state (facial expressions, external reactions) and the external environment of the feedback?
- Write down a few notes about what you're seeing and reflect on what you're learning.

KEY TAKEAWAY

Feedback given in the optimal environment has a greater impact and creates better results.

CHAPTER 6

A Unique Way of Thinking About Feedback

If you change the way you look at things,
the things you look at change.

~Dr. Wayne Dyer

Meg, a CEO of a large company, showed up at our coaching call frustrated with her CFO. He wasn't meeting any of the deadlines that he had set for himself and that they agreed on. Meg's frustration looked like stress and despair but was laced with a bit of embarrassed laughter. I said to Meg, "I can see and experience your stress—what's the laughter about?"

"The situation is ridiculous and I'm not doing anything about it. It's almost as though I expect him not to achieve the results or deadlines."

"Sounds like you're setting a trap."

"No. That's not it. Well, maybe it is. I know he's planning to retire soon. I think that's the reason behind his lack of engagement. The thing is, I don't know when he's planning to retire, so I don't know what to hold him accountable for. And therefore, I'm letting him off the hook."

"What's stopping you from either holding him accountable or from asking him about his retirement date?"

Meg looked down and sighed. "I don't really know. He's been an integral part of our team and I don't want to lose him as a team member. Yet, I know that if nothing changes, I will need to. I guess I am prolonging the inevitable."

"So, this uncertainty is allowing you to play along with his lack of performance and delivering against deadlines and results? Sounds like you're betting against the business by doing this."

Meg looked at me surprised. "No! I'm not betting against the business."

"Really?" I said. "Okay, I'm going to put on my casino dealer's hat and ask you. Now that you've shown me your cards, what card do you want me to deal now?"

We both laughed and I said, "Seriously, Meg. What's your next move? Something's got to change, and we both know it."

Meg said, "You're right. I am going to talk with him during our next one-on-one. I'm going to share with him my observations about missed deadlines, my awareness of his desire to retire, and I'm going to ask him what he would like his legacy to be with the organization—he's been with us for over 25 years."

"Meg, it sounds like you've got clarity about your next moves. I'm looking forward to our next coaching meeting."

———

Twenty years ago, when I first started to train leaders in how to give feedback to inspire their employees and get results back on track, I relied on a script that included helpful videos, checklists on how to "perform" when giving feedback, and the occasional role-play scenario (and we know how much people love those). While this training was valuable, it was essentially a list of directions on how to "do" feedback versus how to "be" with feedback. The trouble with this type of training was that if someone responded in a manner out of alignment with the script, the participant was literally at a loss. Their attachment to the script made it hard for participants to flow with the give-and-take of a feedback session.

When something is scripted, it doesn't provide space or instruction on how to listen to what is being said or to pay attention to the energetics—the body language and tone of voice. The outcome was that these feedback sessions became a robotic exchange of information. Each exchange between the feedback giver and receiver was uncomfortable at best and, in some cases, disastrous. This is because the script didn't allow for the natural organic communication that happens between humans. We weren't teaching the managers how to adapt to the shift in a direction that the feedback conversation might take. The manager was so intent on saying what needed to be said that there wasn't room for listening to how the feedback was being responded to. The result? Meaningful communication is sacrificed.

As I became more immersed in working with organizations, trying to access and deliver more effective ways to give and receive feedback, I learned to take a step back and view the situation with a broader lens. And I started teaching my clients three essential and powerful skills. These include being fully present, listening deeply, and trusting the intuition of useful insights or perspectives.

By being more present and curious, and by asking more questions, you too will gain greater understanding of the context surrounding your employees' needs, and your own. These questions are designed to have you tune into your intuition and to sense the broader context of what needs to happen. This is not a perfect science, but when you become practiced, you'll be amazed by what you can uncover before you provide feedback. And how helpful that is.

- What do I know about the person?
- What do I know about the situation?
- Where do I need clarity?
- What step do I need to take next?
- Who can I unpack the situation with?
- How can I look at the situation from a different place?
- Where do we need to dig deeper?
- Have we been here before?
- What role do I have in this or what role do I need to play?

The more questions I asked and the more skilled I became at asking them, the more the five perspectives or roles, which I call "hats," kept emerging: the Confidante, the Miner, the Pilot, the Historian, and the Visionary. Over time, I realized that each of these roles (hats) used at the appropriate times garnered powerful results. The hat I wear, in other words, changes according to the relationship I have with different leaders, my history with the company, and my reading of the situation. If that sounds a little strange, read on.

I am going to describe these different hats, with the invitation for you to try them on too, to see how they fit you. I am also going to point out how you can use them prior to giving feedback and during feedback. While collaborating with a consultant is valuable, I want you to know how to use these different perspectives to create the optimum foundation from which feedback can be given and received. Most of all, I want you to throw away your rigid scripts and tune into what's happening, recognizing that certain circumstances necessitate different approaches to feedback.

The Confidante (or Coach or Counselor)

This is someone you can confide in, someone you trust with your private thoughts, and who you're sure can keep a secret.

Before feedback: There may be times you need a "confidante," a trusted advisor, coach, or friend to be available to listen to all you feel and have to say, prior to your giving feedback. Confidante creates a safe space for people to get things off their chest, vent frustrations, or complain, and to be completely vulnerable. In doing so, you are clearing your energy (as described in Chapter 4) to ensure you are in the best mental and emotional space to give feedback.

During feedback: When you wear the Confidante hat, you invite a colleague or employee to share what's really going on with them. You remind them it's important you understand their perspective and feelings, before offering your insights or coming up with a plan. This works well when there are tensions between people. Sometimes listening deeply is the best foundation for a successful feedback session. And, like it or not, you are going to learn a lot!

Situations that typically call for the Confidante: When the leader or person has been "hiding out," has some secrets, and/or has been holding back—not addressing issues in a direct manner.

Typical Questions: Tell me more about the person or situation. Where are you holding back? Is there anything else you want to share or that needs to be said? Are you leaving anything out? What do you want to do next? Are you open to my observations or feedback?

Best outcome for this role: Building safety and trust. Allowing the person to be seen, heard, and listened to. Creating an opening to explore what comes next.

Several years ago, I was working with a CEO who recognized his salesperson wasn't performing. The CEO also knew he was reluctant to do anything about it. With my Confidante hat on, I listened to the CEO as he spilled out everything he was feeling. He was frustrated, angry, and upset with the employee and with himself. He was clear that his culture of origin had influenced how he dealt with conflict and was truly afraid to say anything. He was passive by nature and nurture. He talked about how his organizational culture and his personal values stopped him from calling attention to the non-performing employee. The CEO was afraid to hold the employee accountable for the job he hired the person to do. At the same time, the CEO was annoyed that the employee wasn't doing their job, so he was forced to pick up the slack, which took him away from growing the business.

After listening to the CEO share everything that was going on for him, I asked him, "Now that you've gotten all of this off your chest, what role do you want me to play?"

He said, "I really think I need coaching on how to get out of my own way. If I don't learn how to do this, eventually the organization will fail because I couldn't take on dealing with something difficult."

From there, we spent the rest of that meeting and other subsequent meetings working together on building the CEO's competency in addressing tough performance issues and at the same time honoring his values.

The Miner

The Miner is the one who shines the light in dark crevices, looking for gold. The Miner is a seeker, always curious about others and ready to pose questions, as they look for what might lie beneath the surface.

Before feedback: If you aren't sure about what's going on with the person you are about to give feedback to, you may need to spend time in the Miner's role. Reflect on your past relationship with this person—what do you notice? Get curious. Is this an ongoing problem? Did it just start recently? If so, why? What makes this worth pursuing?

It can help to jot down some thoughts, so that you enter the feedback session open, curious, questioning.

During feedback: If appropriate, invite the other person to come along with you, exploring the situation together, so that you are both trying to shine a light on what's going on. The Miner's hat is the perfect one to wear when you sense a problem or issue but aren't sure what's really happening under the surface and so you need to dig deeper.

Situations that typically call for the Miner: When the leader is at a loss or can only see what is on the surface of an employee's behavior. Or when an employee is stuck and can't get out of their own way.

Typical questions: How are you performing? What do you do well in your job? Where can you do better? What's holding you back? Do you have any fears about how you do your job? How do you see your behavior with me and your co-workers? Do you have the right tools and resources to be successful? Where do you want to shine the light? What do you need to explore? How can I help?

Best outcome for this role: To get to the heart of the matter and bring the issues (or the gold) to the surface.

———————

A client contacted me with a sense of urgency that an employee had to be fired. Right away! The client was adamant and mentally prepared to fire the employee. I started to ask questions about the egregious acts of the employee. I asked a lot of questions about the employee and what was missing. I put on my Miner's hat with the intention of digging deep. As I started to ask my questions, my client stepped back, softened, and joined me in exploring what was there. We worked together digging deep until we came up with the right next step for the employee, which wasn't to fire that person, but to give a final warning. At the end of the day, the final warning made all the difference and the employee showed immediate improvement.

The Pilot

The Pilot moves above the "clouds" with the purpose of looking at the full picture—a bird's-eye view of sorts.

Before feedback: In the Pilot role you aren't just looking at the employee, but at how their performance is affecting the whole. This prepares you to see the big picture and put context around why the feedback you are offering is so important to the health of the organization. It also allows you to step back and feel a bit more detached. Like an observer rather than a part of the drama.

During feedback: Inviting the person into the "big view" perspective can help both parties gain clarity, without getting down in the weeds of who did what and whose feelings are hurt. This is about what's good for the company. What's missing that needs to be added, or what's not working. When both the feedback giver and receiver are in Pilot mode, the tone of the meeting can feel very spacious and non-judgmental. You are both in the cockpit navigating toward the most powerful outcome.

Situations that typically call for the Pilot: When someone is too far into the weeds or too close to a situation to be able to see it clearly.

Typical questions: What do you see up here that you did not see down below? What is on the horizon? What do you see from here?

Best outcome for this role: To explore and see things from a "bird's-eye" view. Create distance and explore new outcomes that serve the good of the whole system.

———————————

A client was extremely frustrated with a recent series of decisions being made by his boss, a person he respected. I listened carefully, and then articulated what I heard back to the client and received confirmation that I had heard it right. I told the client that I'd like to explore what he had shared and the impacts of his boss's decisions from a 50,000-foot level. I invited him to join me. As we explored the decisions and impacts from this big perspective place, my client's eyes widened. He said, "I've never thought about this situation this way. I think I have a better way to describe what I'm seeing to my boss. The decisions he's making have much bigger implications than I originally thought, and he needs to know it too. I don't want my boss or the company to fail, and if what I am seeing from here is accurate, the likelihood of a failure is great."

At the end of the session, my client left feeling confident, armed with new insights and the ability to invite his boss on a similar ride.

The Historian

This role can only be assumed when there is some history with the organization or an employee. A historian is the one who keeps a journal of events. They keep a record of significant accomplishments, challenges, and/or performance problems.

Before feedback: Wearing the Historian hat is helpful when preparing for a meeting and you want to have all the facts and figures at your fingertips. I would encourage you to pull out all the information available to assess the history of the employee, such as their past successes and failures as well as previous documented conversations regarding behaviors, projects, successes, and challenges. How often have you been here having a similar conversation? Coming into a meeting prepared will fuel your confidence and can be very empowering.

During feedback: When you are in Historian mode, you can help to remind others what has occurred in the past. You can help them review their patterns of behavior, successes, and/or challenges. When you wear the Historian hat, you are constantly referencing the past, and comparing it with the present. You are aware of the evolving needs of both employees and the company. You aren't just looking at the here and now but are putting it into the context of a longer time frame.

Situations that typically call for the Historian: When a leader needs to review or recall what has happened in the past. When you need to take a historical view. When you want to recognize great performance over a consistent or long period of time. Or when a recurring situation becomes a problem.

Typical questions: Haven't we seen this before? I remember a similar issue occurring six months ago; do you remember it? This feels like a new situation for us, doesn't it? How is this different from the last incident?

Best outcome for this role: To bring to light the fact that the same behaviors or performance patterns are occurring over time. Or, that there's been a change in a behavior or pattern.

For the four years I've worked with him, my client, a CEO, has been talking about the lack of performance of one of his key employees. Every few months, this employee's name comes up. As Historian, I find my notes, share the previous conversations, and ask the CEO what action he would like to take. Every time, the CEO pauses, sighs, and expresses that this employee is like a family member and he won't do anything right now about the lack of performance. While I am a

Historian, I am a Confidante too. I'm holding space for the CEO as he processes his inability to act on the lack of performance, yet again. I am inviting the CEO to look at the history of the conversations we've had on this matter. If I wanted to, I could be assertive and hold the role of an Enforcer for the CEO, and yet the CEO (also founder) is the one who gets to make the decision. I've also learned that making someone do something they aren't ready to do can create resistance.

The Visionary

The Visionary is especially useful during organizational strategic planning sessions. This is where leaders review objectives for the upcoming year with all functional organizations and their leaders.

Before feedback: The Visionary holds some aspects of the Pilot, in that they are often aware of the big picture, but they are more focused on possibilities, fulfilling on mission, or thinking out of the box. Allowing yourself some time to consider where you want your team or organization to be in the year 20XX allows you to step out of the day-to-day tasks for a moment—and dream big. This is an invitation into blue-sky thinking, and it's a key leadership skill.

During feedback: When offering feedback, assuming the Visionary role helps you to motivate those you are giving feedback to, to improve their performance by showing them the potential rewards of such as shift. In this role, you inspire rather than deflate. You encourage rather than disparage. And you invite others into creative brainstorming and yet-to-be imagined possibilities.

Situations that typically call for the Visionary: When an organization and its leaders need to look out into the future, and what they want to accomplish.

Typical questions: "Given the established objectives, do you have the right people to execute the results?" "Do you have the right talent pool?" "What new roles do you need?" "Look out a year from now and ask yourself: Whose skills need to be developed?" "What talent needs to be hired?" "Do people need to shift to different roles inside your organization?" "Imagine we are still here and have accomplished our goals together; what would that make possible?" "How much more engaged would your team be?" "Where do we need to make investments?"

Best outcome for this role: To partner by creating, communicating, and holding a vision for others, setting the tone and expectations.

A client was underachieving. We were meeting in the middle of the second quarter to review the year's goals, and my client was stumped. She leaned over, crossing her arms, head hanging down, and exclaimed, "I'm at a loss. I don't know what to do."

I asked her, "At the beginning of the year, what did you envision for this year?"

My client walked through her vision, her strategy, her plans, and the current results.

I asked her, "Where do you think your gaps are?"

My client leaned back in her chair and said, "I honestly don't know."

I said, "Do you want to take a guess?"

She said, "I don't think my people are performing the way they need to."

I asked the question, "In order to fulfill your vision for your organization, what people on your team are most likely to get you there and which of your employees are derailing progress? Better yet, pretend that we are having this conversation a year from now. What do you wish you had done to stop this from happening?"

My client sat straight up and said clearly, "I have to take a hard look at my employees. Several of them continue to resist the direction that the company is going, and I know that many are not performing their jobs as expected. If I really want to get results, I need to look at a couple of partners and vendors who are not aligned with my vision. If we are sitting here a year from now and my results reflect the same or worse, knowing what I know now, it will have been my fault for not naming what's there and taking action."

From there, sitting side by side, we created a new vision for how her company would achieve the necessary results. She outlined a roadmap of options, created a plan, identified who she needed to include in the process such as her head of Human Resources and her head of Marketing, and devised a few other ideas. Along the way, I continued to hold the role as her Visionary—holding her vision so that she could see it more clearly as she mapped out what was next.

THOUGHTS ON FEEDBACK

What Is the Purpose of a Hat?

One of the first pictorial depictions of a hat appears in a tomb painting in Thebes, Egypt, which shows a man wearing a conical straw hat, dated to around 3200 BCE. Hats were originally created for protective purposes to keep our heads and faces shielded from the sun. Over the years, they have become an important fashion accessory and an outward expression of ceremony, for religious reasons, safety, and fashion. Wearing a hat is also a way to adopt a new persona.

You might be asking yourself, "Do I really need to assume one of these roles to give feedback?" The answer is, "No." You can turn up as the person you are in the role you play in an organization and very much as yourself. But what I have learned is that when you put on one of these hats, you are able to shift your thinking and explore new territory. The "hats" allow you the freedom to step outside of yourself to realize what is needed for the occasion for the greater good and a more deliberate outcome. Role-playing can also take you out of a more ego-driven state. It allows you to ask yourself, "What and who do I need to be now to create an optimal result?" Both before and during a feedback session, you can ask yourself, "Given what I know, does this meeting call for me to be a Miner or a Pilot, or another role?" From this point, you can then choose not only the "hat" or role, but the outcome you would like to achieve.

Again, the importance of accessing different roles is for you to see and experience new things by taking on a different perspective. The goal is to both strengthen your leadership and your relationships with others.

Here's another thought: What if you approached every encounter or meeting with the simple internal and conscious inquiry of, "Who do I need to be?" or "What role do I need to play?" or "How do I want to show up?" If you're like other leaders I work with, you'll find that using these simple inquiries creates a certain mindset on how you want to behave, as well as how you can influence how others receive and perceive you.

If you don't always create that level of intention or consciousness prior to meeting with someone, you can use the same questions flipped around at the end of the day. "Who was I today?" or "What roles did I take on today?" or "How did I show up today?" Along with one of those questions, you might also add, "Was I effective? How did I connect with each interaction? Is there anything I missed?"

When I work with leaders, either one on one or in facilitated learning sessions, I encourage them to use these questions daily.

What I have found is that these simple and meaningful questions can completely shift a leader's confidence in themselves and their team, and can help to create new relationships with their employees. In my experience, applying these questions regularly will quickly reward you with insights into how to get the best out of yourself and your team.

Operating out of rigid perspectives limits and narrows how we see things. Trying on different hats allows you to look at a situation and person in multiple different ways. They help to activate your imagination, allowing you to see things you couldn't see before, and eliciting comments and responses that wouldn't have been previously possible.

If part of you is still thinking, "How does trying on different 'hats' help me identify which role I am going to play when giving feedbaack?" Then I want you to know that whether you consciously choose to adopt a role or not, you will fall into one or another anyway. More often than not, those unconsciously chosen roles—such as the Judge, the Punisher, the Victim—aren't helpful. But when you consciously choose a helpful perspective, you raise the level of what's possible with feedback. You create an exchange that is illuminating and respectful. Most importantly, you "de-personalize" your feedback, moving away from the "you did this to me" attitude to "you know, from the place of the Historian, I can see we've covered this terrain before. What do you think is going on?" By adopting this practice, you'll be surprised by how quickly performance and relationships positively shift.

It is frequently helpful to invite the person you will be giving feedback to into that role with you. For example, you might say to someone you work with, "Let's look at the situation through the lens that a pilot might see."

Getting comfortable wearing these different hats will take practice, time, and a little imagination. That said, using these tools will guarantee you are on the same journey with those you need to provide feedback to. This will also help you and others to cultivate meaningful relationships and connections. And, if your experience is anything like mine, you'll find that putting on a hat is liberating, allowing you to play, imagine, and create as part of a feedback session, instead of getting tangled up in your own fears or energy blocks.

Other hats or roles to play could be a Sailboat Captain. "Where did we go off course?" Or a Football Coach. "How did we fumble?" The Teacher: "What lessons can we learn here?" Or, "What areas of your job do you need more support with?" I would encourage you to use your own imagination and come up with metaphors that work most effectively for you.

What I love about considering different hats or roles is that it takes us out of the context of how "hard" giving feedback can be and invites us to start from a place of curiosity and understanding. What's necessary for optimum performance or behavior? What is getting in the way? This open, curious stance creates a pathway to explore how to improve, instead of just drawing attention to the problem or shortcoming. It also helps to cultivate genuine and connected relationships. While I wish there were a one-step approach in giving feedback, the reality is there just isn't. Human beings are incredibly creative, resourceful, messy, and complex. One approach does not fit all situations for optimum and continuous growth and development.

By reading this chapter, you will have learned that there are multiple ways to look at and explore a feedback situation. You will have gained relevant examples of roles you can try out and take with you. Like anything, practice makes perfect. If you can learn to experiment with these "hats" while remaining open to learning what each can teach you, very soon you will have transformed your relationship to feedback from one of dread to one in which you feel secure and empowered. And hats off to you!

REFLECTIONS / PRACTICES

When you think of giving feedback, which of the hats appeal to you?

What other new hats have you thought of that you could try out when giving feedback?

Challenge:

Go to a store that sells hats and try a few on. What persona do you embody by trying on that hat?

KEY TAKEAWAY

Approaching feedback from one perspective can limit our ability to become artful at this key skill. When you think about it playfully, as if you're wearing different hats, it can open you to creative solutions and leverage the feedback even more effectively.

CHAPTER 7

Why Feedback Is Core to Leadership

A leader takes people where they want to go.
A great leader takes people where they don't
necessarily want to go, but ought to be.

~Rosalynn Carter

A few years ago in late December, one of my clients, an SVP of Sales, showed up for our meeting ecstatic about the year he just had. Thrilled with the accomplishments of his team, he exclaimed, "I'm so happy with how this year went, I don't want to move into the new year without taking some time to reflect on and to thank those on my team who made this happen. Without the efforts of everyone, we couldn't have accomplished this much success. It truly took the team to create these results."

"Congratulations! I'm thrilled for you and the team," I responded. "Have you taken any time to capture and recap the results?"

"No. I haven't. Not really."

"Would you like to use some of our time together to gather your thoughts and words?"

"Yes." He took a few deep breaths, rubbed his hand across his fore-head and down his beard, and took a few more deep breaths.

"Wow, I am simply grateful. We blew past our plan—way past it. I couldn't be happier."

"I can see your smile. What's in your heart right now?"

"It's full. So full. I'm in awe of my team and what they accomplished. They beat the odds, supported one another, and really listened to the customers' needs. It was like magic. Everything just flowed."

"What made this year different from the others?"

"You know what? I've been different this year. The biggest dif-ference for me is I've stepped back from controlling everyone and everything. I've learned to lean in and listen to my team. I've been more curious and collaborative with everyone, even my boss. I also know that I was clear about asking for what results I wanted. And I gave clear feedback when I saw something was off. This year has been markedly different than all my other years at work. My health is better too. My blood pressure over the past six months has been the lowest it's been in years. A lot of this has to do with our coach-ing work together. While I was resistant at first, I'm grateful. Thank you. Would you mind if I draft my email or maybe 'script' of what I want to share with each member of the team while we're together? Perhaps you can provide me with feedback?"

I answered with a hearty, "It would be great to use our time this way. Yes, I'm here—just let me know when you'd like input or feedback."

He worked through what he wanted to say, and when finished, sat back and said, "That feels so good! I can't wait to talk with the team. Most times, I'm asking for and pushing for more. I'm glad that we took this time so that I could get grounded and really clear on how I want to celebrate with the team. There's more I will do with them, but for now, this is a great start. Thanks for this time."

Leading people is serious business. Leaders play one of the most important roles in organizations today, and are responsible not only for their own goals, results, and development, but for those of the people that report to them. In other words, leaders are responsible for other people's productivity and work success.

When you step into the role of a leader, you willingly choose to accept the rewarding and tough parts of helping to grow and cultivate others. Providing feedback is part of this often-spoken agreement that lies at the heart of leadership.

Many of my coaching clients started their careers in traditional hierarchical organizations. They were groomed to be the "tough guys" or "aggressive, no-nonsense women." I certainly grew up in the corporate world when the boss was supposed to have all the answers, know best, and not be questioned. This was a top-down approach to organizational design with a rigid pecking order. Decisions were made by the higher-ups, and communication trickled down to employees only when it was necessary to furnish information and instructions. Input was seldom asked for and "falling in line" was required.

Regardless of the leadership structure and the title of a person, when someone is being too tough, direct, or abrasive with others, they are shutting the door on forming relationships with people they work with or who work for them. Without forming meaningful relationships with peers and employees, these leaders remain shut off from what was really going on around them. The result? They often push people away and encourage office gossip by upsetting and alienating employees. The reality is that a "bully of a boss" doesn't encourage people to work harder. Quite the opposite occurs. Employees spend more hours in a day quietly complaining among themselves.

Today, many organizations, while still employing a top-down structural approach, have also implemented open channels of communication to allow for a richer flow of information. Information is not only encouraged and directed from the top down, but side to side and bottom up. Leading industry organizations understand the value of decentralizing decisions by inviting input, insights, and feedback from all areas of the organization. The value of deeper connections, greater alignment, and increased commitment between peers is becoming more apparent. Creating bottom-up communication inspires employees to participate in solving problems, making decisions, and providing feedback. The open flow of communication is critical to employee engagement, motivation, and loyalty and creates ownership. Employees today haven't been trained to follow a leader blindly. They value collaboration and know they can share their voice. Inviting perspectives, insights, and feedback from all levels ensures that the topic at hand is given its due diligence from a variety of perspectives and includes others' input. Who knows better about customer experience, for example, than the person who is dealing with the customer day in and day out?

While organizational structure and design is important, ensuring that leaders have the right skills to cultivate meaningful and connected cultures is critical.

Jess had been newly promoted to lead a team that was comprised of former peers. He was excited to be stepping into a management position. During our coaching session, Jess told me that one of his guys hadn't listened to directions and messed up an order, costing the organization thousands of dollars. Jess had reacted by snapping at the employee: "What's wrong with you? It's clear you aren't listening to my instructions. I take time telling you what to do. And then you mess up like this. Frankly, you are wasting my time."

My initial internal reaction was "Ouch. That was a bit harsh. Most people I know would either experience that statement as a "shove" or a "challenge."

I slowed down, dug deep, and took a risk. I looked at my client and said, "You know what, Jess, you messed up, and you are wasting my time."

The look on his face was both priceless and painful. I hated what I saw. And at the same time, I waited and allowed his words, as I mirrored them back, to wash over him. As they did, there it was. He experienced what he had put his employee through. Mission accomplished. The room was silent for one... two... three... four... five seconds.

Jess looked at me, dropped his head in his hands, and said, (Expletive!) He sat back, looked at the ceiling, inhaled, and then exhaled deeply. "That hurt."

"What hurt?" I asked.

"Your words. They cut deep. And they were my words. Damn. I messed up with this guy. He's a kid new to his job."

"Now what?" I asked.

"I need to fix this. I didn't mean that. Not really. I care about the guy. He's a good person doing the best he can."

"And what else?" I asked.

"I was just being a tough guy, like I was the 'boss' or something. And I am the boss." Silence. "And I don't know what I'm doing. Crap. I really want to be a good manager. I think I was kind of showing off or something."

We sat in silence for a minute.

"So now what?" I asked.

Jess looked at me for a few long seconds and said, "How do I do this?"

I asked, "What do you want to do?"

Jess said, "How do I deal with the situation with my guy?"

I said, "What is the near-term end result that you'd like with this person?"

Jess said, "Honestly, I want him to slow down, listen, and follow instructions. He is costing the company money, and every time he messes up, it has an impact on me, the organization, and the customer. I'm then forced to explain to my manager why we are spending more money on the project; not only that, but I have to get involved with the customer and fix the mess. All of this is taking valuable time that I already don't have."

I asked, "And what else?"

Jess thought for a few seconds and answered, "I'd like for this employee to develop and grow so that I can trust him with more complicated jobs."

I asked, "Anything else?"

Jess said, "I don't want the feedback I provide to him in the future to be so harsh. He doesn't deserve that—he's just learning."

"Okay, here's what I hear you saying. You would like to deliver feedback to your employee in a way that he hears it, and that encourages him to slow down, listen, and understand the impact of what he's doing. You want him to learn. You also want to create a relationship where he feels free to ask questions so that he can learn his job, grow, and be counted on in the future. Is that right?"

"Yes, that's pretty much it," said Jess.

"Great!" I said, "I have a simple tried and tested approach I'd like to share with you. The model is SBI™ and I'd like to add an E. It stands for:

- S=Situation
- B=Behavior
- I=Impact
- E=Explore, Examine, Expect

"Using this model, how can you construct a conversation with your employee?"

From there, Jess explored and practiced a few ways that he could use this model to craft a new message with his employee.

To help illustrate the use of the SBI™ model, created by the Center for Creative Leadership (CCL), I am going to use one of Jess' practice examples:

Situation: I'd like to follow up with you on the situation that happened a few weeks ago. The one where we had to reorder the right parts for the job we were close to completing for our customer. How I responded to that situation was reactive, and now I'd like to provide you with feedback on what happened because of that situation.

Behavior: I have noticed a pattern of behavior you exhibit when I provide you with guidance and instruction, and that is that you aren't fully listening. I see you nodding your head even before I get any words out and saying "Yeah, I understand" before I finish writing down the specs for the job. What this indicates to me is that you're moving too fast and not fully listening. Is that a fair statement?

Impact: When you move fast and don't fully listen, the impact is that we skip over critical details and information, resulting in placing wrong orders. By ordering the wrong parts, we cost the company more money, we have a delay in the job, the customer isn't happy, and we are at risk of losing a customer who could potentially find another vendor. I also have to explain to my boss what happened. If these types of errors continue to occur, there may be an impact on your employment, which I would hate to see. I really value you as an employee.

Explore, Examine, Expect: How can you slow down, listen, and follow instructions more carefully? What support do you need from me? What consequences do you think should occur if these errors continue?

As you wrap up a conversation using the model above, you can conclude with, "Do you fully understand the situation, behavior, and impact? What are you willing to commit to? Is there anything else I need to know?"

This type of conversation is direct and clear and invites an environment of openness and curiosity that unlocks the mind and heart. It also creates the opportunity for the employee to own his/her behavior and understand how it impacts overall performance and results for the company.

The next time we got together, Jess shared with me that he apologized to his employee for his initial reaction. He explained that the feedback he gave him was disrespectful and that he wouldn't react that way in the future. Jess told me that he used the model I introduced. Not only did it help the employee understand the situation better, but it also created a better, more compassionate, and connected relationship between Jess and his employee.

What Jess shared with me is that when he stopped trying to be the "tough guy" leader, his employee felt more comfortable telling him things and asking questions. The work relationship rested on a stronger foundation. Jess found that he was also using this same model in working through some issues with his teenage sons. As he said to me," I'm using every opportunity I can to practice using this model. It's so simple and effective."

As you wrap up a conversation using the SBI-E model above, you can conclude with, "Do you fully understand the situation, behavior, and impact? What are you willing to commit to? Is there anything else I need to know?"

In the book *Crucial Conversations: Tools for Talking When Stakes Are High*, authors Kerry Patterson, Ron McMillian, and Al Switzer introduce the concept of Start with Heart. The idea is to begin with the right motives in mind and state what you really want (in the relationship, as an outcome on a project, etc.) and to do so with curiosity and not the need to be "right."

THOUGHTS ON FEEDBACK

65 percent of Employees Desire More Feedback

According to Zippia.com, an organization that helps people further their careers, employees desire more feedback than they're getting, which means that leaders are not providing sufficient feedback on a regular basis. On the other hand, 43 percent of highly engaged employees receive feedback at least once a week. Feedback doesn't just improve results, it helps retain talent. And it's your job to provide it.

After Chuck, the CEO, had provided timely and critical feedback to one of his key leaders, a VP named Bob, he told me, "One of the things I have learned in my years of leading people is that humans are fragile. I needed to deliver a tough message to Bob that was timely, clear, direct, and kind. Giving feedback is about stepping into an uncomfortable situation, knowing that through the experience we will both grow."

Even though Chuck was the company's new CEO, only on board for a few weeks, he recognized he was accountable for all business results through leading and managing others. Bob, the VP, was responsible for the delivery of key financial results through the professional services the business provides. What concerned Chuck was that for four months the division under Bob's leadership had not met their business and financial goals. After "pulling back the curtain" to examine "why," it was clear that Bob hadn't established a clear strategy, objectives, or goals. That, coupled with the fact that Bob wasn't holding regular one-on-one, team, or other meetings with his direct reports and staff caused Chuck concern. In speaking with Bob, Chuck learned that Bob was "too busy" to perform these critical leadership responsibilities.

After providing constructive feedback to Bob, Chuck told Bob that he wanted him to be successful and was available to support his development. However, he was not willing to allow missed results and a clear absence of leadership to continue.

Bob told Chuck that the feedback was BS. Chuck responded, "You may feel that way, but your results speak for themselves."

Chuck asked Bob to take a few days to think about his role, the situation, and what he was willing to do to step up and perform as required.

What I appreciate about Chuck is his awareness that there is never a perfect or easy time to provide tough feedback. It's a bit of a dance. And yet he didn't avoid it. He understood the necessity and purpose of the feedback. He wasn't fearful. But he was also kind, his intentions were good, and his timing was as right as it would ever be.

When I met with Chuck two weeks after the feedback session, he shared that Bob had told him he spent the first weekend angrily considering whether he would stay with the company or not. After thinking about it and talking through the situation with people he trusted, Bob confirmed with Chuck that he wanted to stay with the organization. Bob further went on to share with Chuck that at this point in his career, he needed someone who was willing to invest in him for the long term. He was about ten years away from retirement and didn't want to "blow it" now. Additionally, as Bob opened up, he shared with Chuck that as he had risen in his position of leadership, no one had ever given him *direct feedback or invested in or developed his skills in the role. Quite frankly, Bob said, he was uncertain about his position as a leader. He knew deep down that he needed help, coaching, support, and training to fully learn, own, and commit to the role he had chosen to accept. He told Chuck he was ready to get to work.*

———————————

In this case, the intended feedback was delivered and received, and a new plan was created for moving forward.

Chuck's ability to deliver this type of message didn't just happen overnight. When I first met him, he told me that he took this leadership role very seriously. He read several leadership books a year and regularly practiced the tools he learned, not always getting it right or perfect, but knowing that to be better every day, he needed to practice the skills and drills. What's more, Chuck learned a lot about the "Why" of feedback. He knew why he was offering it and had the mindset he needed to get the outcomes he was looking for.

Developing Your Growth Mindset

As we've been exploring, there are many ways to go about giving feedback, and yet all of them share a common need to get clear on your inner state and your external objectives. Another lens we can look through is that of motivation—the big "Why" at the heart of feedback. To begin, I'm going to invite you to think through any recent feedback you have provided. What was your motivation for providing that feedback? Was the feedback because you wanted something? Or was it because you wanted something for them? Neither is wrong. Or right for that matter. Mostly, it's a mix of both, but it's helpful to consider whether your motivation was YOU focused or THEM focused. So here are some questions to ask yourself:

- Do you want their behavior to change? If so, why?
- Do you want them to grow in their role? If so, why?
- Do you want them to do what you want? If so, why?
- Do you want them to develop? If so, why?
- Do you want to prove that you are right about something? If so, why?

Take a few minutes and really consider the person you provided feedback to and what your motivation was to provide the feedback. Does it include a concern for the development and betterment of your colleagues and employees? Or perhaps it's a little more self-serving? In other words, it's about covering your tracks and making sure you look good. No shame here; we need to protect our careers too. But the reality is that as leaders, we are also tasked with the well-being of those who work for us. Take a moment to reflect on your answers. They may provide just the important insights you need on where your focus lies with your employees.

During my introductory story when I experienced Marc's feedback, I said that I would share something with you in relation to leadership and having the right resources on the team. What I didn't say back then is that this is also a story about thinking about others.

————————————

Back then I led twenty-five employees, directly and indirectly, in the learning and development department of a large company. Marc, as you may recall, said I was putting the team and organization at risk by taking on all the projects. During that time, I had asked my boss to hire more employees. He asked me to evaluate those I already had on staff first—the best course of action. My role was to ensure that I had the right employees to support the organization at that time. I believed I had 96 percent of the right resources. They were committed, thorough, and talented. They got the job done.

One of my employees, though, was a "work in progress" in my eyes. I could see his potential and some growth. But he was not a "fast walker" as my boss would say. My boss perceived him as biding his time and presenting unprofessionally. Both were true. What this employee was able to do that my boss couldn't see was relate to people who worked in the field, on the line, and in the homes while installing telecommunication services. From my lens, this employee wasn't someone who would train professional sales employees, but he was darn good at training the people who would interact with those responsible for installing our services in homes.

In many ways it would have been easier to have gotten rid of the problematic employee and acquired a new hire. But firing someone is a big deal. And this person had talent in an area that would have been underserved without him. Because I wasn't only focused on ME, but the good of the team and the other employees, I was able to offer him feedback about how he needed to show up more professionally at work and how much I valued his contributions as field operations trainer. In the end, it was a win-win. This person cleaned up his act, kept his job, and we continued to benefit from his particular skill set.

Your underlying motivation in providing feedback contributes to your mindset. If you are thinking of others and the greater good, you will be less likely to eliminate someone of value because they aren't everything you want them to be—yet. Like Chuck with his VP, like me with my "work in progress" employee, having a Growth Mindset allows you to find solutions that can work for all parties concerned. Let's take a deeper dive into Mindset by looking at Figure 11.

Giver of Feedback

Fixed Mindset = Criticism	Growth Mindset = Feedback
This person just doesn't know how to do their job. What a moron. I should just fire this person.	This person isn't performing well; I wonder what is going on?
I knew this person wasn't going to be able to do what's needed in this job.	I can see this person isn't doing their best work and I want them to be successful. I need to talk with them and see where they need help.
Oh brother, I don't want to deal with this person's challenges. I wish this situation or person would just go away.	I care about this person and want them to thrive in their work and environment.
Why can't this person just improve? Can't s/he see how much they are failing?	I should provide feedback to this person. It's possible this person is unaware of their weakness.
This person has been employed with us for a month and just isn't performing as we expected. Metrics are low; I should just fire them. It's been 30 days, right?	I'm really surprised this person isn't being successful. During the interview I was certain they were a good fit. I should provide feedback on what we are observing and ask if s/he needs more training and to see what is missing to get this person in a successful spot.

FIGURE 11

Take a moment and consider how you think about the people on your team. Do you tend to have a fixed mindset or a growth mindset when considering their performance? How is either mindset serving you, your team, or the organization? I would encourage you to track your thoughts over the course of an upcoming week. Every time you notice that someone isn't doing their job as expected, where does your mind wander? Do you simply want to criticize them? Or do you want to grow them?

Take the following example.

I was in a meeting with a CEO and his head of marketing. They were discussing an employee who had been with the company for six months. It was the employee's first job out of college, and the employee was disengaged. Not the "happy" person who arrived on the first day of employment. While the two leaders were discussing their perceptions about the employee, I had an opportunity to observe their language (both body and verbal). They were saying things like, "I knew it would turn out this way; we shouldn't have taken a risk on a recent grad. They don't even know what they're doing." It was clear they had already "quit on the employee." What was also clear, based on what they were discussing, is that the employee hadn't done anything "wrong" or "bad" per se. The employee just wasn't delivering the expected results and wasn't showing up engaged. The employee was what I would call stagnant, or "meh."

After listening to the two of them talk, I asked the question, "What type of training have you provided this employee?"

The CEO looked to the head of marketing for a response. The head of marketing responded, "The new hire told us they had the experience needed to do the job. We provided onboarding, shared the tools we used, and put the employee to work."

I asked, "What feedback, guidance, or coaching have you provided the employee?"

The head of marketing said, "We really haven't. In my book, it takes too much time. I've chosen to rely on another person in the department to show that person what to do, and if that doesn't work, to pick up and do the work that I originally hired this person to do."

I asked, "So what is the employee doing all day while at work?"

The head of marketing said, "I'm not entirely sure. I know that the person is here during work hours. What are they doing? I don't really know. I don't interact with that person very much."

I looked at the CEO and the head of marketing and said, "So, let me clarify what I just heard. Six months ago, you hired a college graduate with the expectation that this person would perform a particular job. After this person was on board for a while and was not completing the tasks and responsibilities required to be successful, you asked someone else on the team to either show that person what to do or pick up that person's work. You haven't provided feedback, guidance, coaching, or training over the past few months. Is this right?"

The head of marketing said, "Yes. That's about it. We just don't have the time to train someone to bring them up to speed."

At this point, I could see that the CEO looked surprised by what she was hearing.

I then asked both, "Imagine that it's twenty years from now and this employee is talking about their first professional work experience out of college. What would you hope they would say?"

The CEO said, "I would hope that they would say that this was a great experience for them and that they grew in their role." The head of marketing was visibly squirming at this point.

I asked, "What intentional influence do you have on that outcome right now? In other words, how will you engage with the employee who is 'stalled' in a manner to create this imaginary outcome? This isn't necessarily the employee's issue to fix. You two are the leaders. Rather than sitting in here talking about the employee, why not pull the employee into the conversation with the purpose of discovering what is going on rather than making up stories about what you think is going on? The only person who can tell you what needs to be fixed is the person that isn't here. I would also pull in the right people to figure out how to get this person trained to be successful, and fast. My concern for both of you is you are losing credibility in addition to valuable dollars each day that this person isn't productive and doesn't feel successful. So, let's create an action plan to move forward . . ."

Don't get me wrong. Sometimes it is important to pull someone from the "game." But in the scenario above, I didn't think that was the case. The CEO and head of marketing needed to reset the clock if the employee hadn't already completely checked out. So, let me ask you, what would you do in that situation? Or have you found yourself in a similar situation, and how did you respond? And would you respond differently now?

The next example is an elegant and practical way to look at when it's time to give feedback and/or perhaps pull someone from the "game."

In 2016, in Oprah Winfrey's Super Soul Sunday interview with the CEO of LinkedIn, Jeff Weimer, Oprah and Jeff discussed the importance of leadership. Oprah focused on a statement made by Jeff that one of the biggest mistakes a leader can make is leaving people in positions they are no longer suited for. Compassion means sometimes transitioning a person out of their role or even the company. Jeff goes on to say using a baseball metaphor, "The most important thing I've learned about being a CEO is not to leave the pitcher in the game too long."

He goes on to describe that it's the manager's role to check on the "pitcher;" in this case, to see how that person is doing. Most often the "pitcher" will say, "I've got it. I'm fine. Go sit down." Jeff continues, "Most people assume that compassion means not making hard decisions, not making hard choices, not transitioning employees out of roles, and it's the exact opposite. The least compassionate thing you can do when someone is not equipped for the task is to leave them in their role." Later in the interview, Jeff says, "The most compassionate thing you can do is to take the person aside and say, this isn't working out right now. Here's where the bar is set. I'm going to do everything I can to get you to the bar or above the bar. But we're going to set a timetable." Oprah finishes his sentence by saying, "Or, *we're going to have to let you go." Jeff agrees and provides a little more context prior to the interview conclusion.*

As I mentioned before, leading people is serious business. It is by far one of the most important and impactful roles in any company. Leaders set the stage for success for all of those around them. While leaders are not 100 percent responsible for the complete success of their employees, how leaders "show up" every day in their roles has a significant influence on everyone else. Leaders are in fact responsible for setting their employees up to perform to the best of their abilities.

If you are in a leadership role, I hope you realize that you have willingly, if not consciously, chosen to accept all that being a leader entails. And that includes guiding, coaching, growing, and cultivating others. Providing feedback is part of the package.

REFLECTIONS / PRACTICES

Think about and/or take notes or journal about someone you need to give feedback to:

- Who is the person to you?
- What do you know about this person?
- Is there any fear you are experiencing by giving this feedback? What is it?
- What is the purpose of providing this feedback (i.e., behavior change, mistake correction)?
- What is the feedback you want to/need to give? Be clear and succinct.
- What is the outcome you'd like to achieve by giving this feedback?

- When will you give this feedback to this person (I'm being your accountability buddy, here)?

KEY TAKEAWAY

Not only is feedback important in our working relationships and output, but it is also a skill that can instantly strengthen the integrity, power, and performance of someone in a leadership role. Leading with feedback, when executed with care, is one of the best things a leader can do.

CHAPTER 8

Things that Get in the Way of Giving Feedback

We can choose courage or we can choose comfort,
but we can't have both. Not at the same time.

~Brené Brown

According to a 2022 Gallup study, when employees receive meaningful feedback, they are almost four times more likely than other employees to be engaged at work. Despite several studies and the proven benefits of feedback, 65 percent of employees do not feel they receive regular feedback, and if regular feedback is provided, 78 percent of workers report being more motivated in their jobs.

If feedback is so critical to motivation, engagement, and retention of employees, why isn't it being provided more frequently?

What Gets in the Way of Providing Feedback?

Ourselves. Yep. Every day. We get in our own way.

Throughout my career, I have encountered thousands of leaders and others who long for the ability to provide feedback. While not scientifically researched, approximately 80 percent of people I've encountered get in their own way in providing feedback. There are a lot of reasons for this, some of which I've mentioned previously and will restate now. Recurring and recycled thoughts include: "What will I say?" "How will I say it?" "What if I get it wrong?" "What if they get mad?" "What if they quit?" "Maybe it will resolve itself. I'll wait to see if it happens again." The list goes on and on and on.

The fact is, when we provide feedback, we have a higher chance of getting what we want (i.e., to generate better outcomes, relationships, results, and connection). If we don't provide feedback, likely we won't get the results we want.

A recent exercise I've used with leaders is what I call the Sandwich Exercise. Imagine you stop at a restaurant for a sandwich. In looking at the menu, you see a turkey, avocado, and bacon sandwich on the menu. Everything that is being provided on the sandwich sounds good except you don't like bacon, tomatoes, or onions. And you'd prefer the gluten-free bread option as opposed to the croissant that's mentioned on the menu. When it's time to order the sandwich, are you explicit about the way you would like it prepared (no bacon, tomatoes, or onions, hold the croissant, and prepare it on gluten-free bread)? Or do you order it just as the menu states? When the sandwich is delivered and you're eating it, are you satisfied with the outcome? If you're not satisfied, do you ask for something else? Or do you quietly accept it as it is and give yourself a silent reminder to never return to the restaurant?

I use this Sandwich Exercise to help leaders see just how ineffective it is to hold back on feedback. It also takes them out of only thinking about the workplace in order to check in on other non-work-related habits or tendencies to see if there is a bigger pattern. I get mixed results from leaders and their responses. Some leaders are adamant about requesting and getting what they want, even if it embarrasses those around them (several leaders laugh and say that their kids have lots of memories of these experiences). Some leaders will visibly blanch, saying, "I seldom get what I want in restaurants as I'll generally accept the food as it's advertised." From here, I'll spend time unpacking that behavior and see how it ties into work-related examples.

If You Don't Have Anything Nice to Say

Have you ever heard the phrase, "If you don't have anything nice to say, don't say anything"? My mom used that one a lot. And for a long time, I made it mean that I couldn't express what I didn't like. I would ignore or shy away from telling someone that they hurt my feelings or something as simple as I don't like my vegetables cooked a certain way. I would just take things as they were. I buried a lot of what I wanted and was important to me. In keeping my mouth shut, I found that I built up a lot of resentment. Even worse, by not sharing what I thought, I sometimes gossiped or complained about another person. Not to the person who could fix the complaint, mind you, but someone who would side with me and support the fact that I was right, or I was being mistreated. My hyper-critical, judgmental self had a lot to say, and being an extrovert, I needed to say it out loud to someone who would listen. But here's the thing, that person couldn't change anything about the situation.

The truth is (and I love you, Mom), that phrase is just nonsense. We should be teaching our children and everyone around us to share their truth about what they see, experience, and want through building communication skills that create connection, not separation. Feedback, delivered from that place of connection, helps to build confidence and relationships. Sharing your truth doesn't mean you have to be a jerk about it. There are ways to share feedback in a mindful, respectful, and compassionate manner.

Several years ago, I was brought into an organization by Taylor, a leader who wanted me to coach her leadership team to be more proactive. She professed that they rarely took the initiative in offering new ideas or approaches, and she often felt in meetings that if she wasn't speaking, then they'd end up sitting in silence. This left her feeling isolated and as if everything rested on her shoulders.

Early in my engagement, I met with a few leaders (including Taylor) and employees from various departments who were coming together to discuss an issue that had arisen with their customer experience. The organization was seeing an increase in customer dissatisfaction and not sure why. Taylor quickly took charge, and then invited the others to offer their input. The first person made a suggestion, and Taylor visibly dismissed them and their idea as unworkable. After a few moments of awkward silence, Taylor, visibly frustrated, said, "Hey, this is a brainstorming session—all ideas are welcome." Someone else perked up, and before they could finish what they were saying, Taylor interrupted, "We've (expletive) already looked at that—it's a no-go." The meeting wrapped up thirty minutes early.

I knew Taylor to be talented, caring, passionate, and respected. But this was something new. I hadn't seen this level of aggressiveness or control from her before. I saw the discomfort on those attending that meeting, and I sympathized with them. It was like every time they opened their mouths, they were cut down. People wanted to escape the meeting as soon as possible. Perhaps to review their resumes?

After that meeting, I found that I had two choices. One, I could ignore what had happened and hope that it was a momentary aberration. The second choice was to provide feedback to Taylor on the direct juxtaposition of what I observed and what I knew Taylor wanted to create, which was a collaborative work environment.

Sounds so easy, right? Obviously the second choice is the right one. To be honest, I was experiencing a little hesitancy in providing this feedback to my client. While passion and aggression may drive the company or leadership team well, it can be intimidating to a coach. And I knew I could be cut off just as easily as those in the meeting had been. And yet, providing feedback to Taylor was the only option I saw to be in alignment with Taylor's coaching requests. Taylor wanted to ensure that the leadership team members were less passive and more proactive. And my job was to provide coaching and development to ensure that the company's needs were met. So, here's what happened.

I called Taylor and said, "Hi, Taylor, do you have a minute?"

Taylor said, "Yep. What's up?"

I said, "Taylor, we've worked together for a while. I know that you're committed to the leadership team stepping up and speaking out, and you hired me to ensure that this happened. I noticed something during our last meeting that I'd like to share with you."

Taylor said, "Yep. What?"

I said, "You expressed your frustration with every idea presented, even using several curse words and interrupting before people had completed their thoughts. Do you remember?"

Taylor said, "Yep. Why?"

I said, "I really value working with you and the team on developing a more collaborative and creative culture. From my perspective, you were the one that was preventing that from happening. You shamed people for doing what you asked. This wasn't a brainstorming session. And your language was inappropriate."

Taylor said, "Is that what you had to say?"

I said, "Yes. That's it."

Taylor said, "Unf#$ing believable. Got it. Bye."*

After Taylor hung up, I chuckled for a few minutes at the irony of her cursing, but also was relieved not to have been cut off before I had my say. But what was I supposed to do with her response?

The answer is: trust it. Trust that the feedback is "soaking in." Let the dust settle. The person who receives feedback has permission to take it in. To let the feedback envelop them for a minute (or an hour) or more. Whether it's new or has been heard before, most often and regardless of role, people need to examine, explore, and process feedback before they respond.

I never heard back directly from Taylor on that feedback. And that's okay. Sometimes, when we provide feedback to people, we expect them to come back to us with words of affirmation, agreement, or questions. What I've learned with feedback is that actions speak louder than words. And what I did observe was that Taylor was much more respectful of others' input, at least when I was around and attending meetings. And I never heard her swear at anyone again. Other leaders validated that Taylor was less aggressive in her delivery, and more open to suggestions. It was reported that the office atmosphere was less tense. I continued to focus my coaching and development with the leadership team, working with them to step into their positions of leadership more powerfully, which proved to be a worthwhile investment.

At the end of the day, I'm not attached to people changing their behavior. I'm committed to shining a light on what might be getting in their way of being the best version of themselves. If a different path is chosen, so be it.

Criticism or Feedback?

Most people I know are hyper self-critical, with an internal feedback machine that runs 24/7. We think thoughts like, "I could have done that better." Or "Why didn't I think of that before?" Or "I'm so stupid." Or "I'm going to be late. They're going to be mad at me." The list can go on and on. Being overly critical of ourselves relates to our own insecurities. That said, people who are self-judgmental tend to be overly critical of others too. It's how we make ourselves feel better about who we think we are. If someone else is truly messing up, then our little mess-ups can't be so bad. So be sure to check in with yourself. Are you disparaging someone else's performance to hide your own shame or self-judgment? And don't judge yourself if you are. We are all culpable of doing this at times. But we can all learn to do better. And we must.

According to Rick Hanson, Ph.D., author of *Hardwiring Happiness*, our brains are wired toward the negativity bias. Based on his studies and observations, Dr. Hanson states the brain acts like Velcro with negative experiences and thoughts, versus Teflon for positive experiences and thoughts. Dr. Hanson goes on to share throughout his book that our brains are wired specifically to be on high alert for danger—we're either being hunted or hunting, which puts us in a stress response. Although human society and culture have evolved beyond the hunting-gathering days, our brain response hasn't evolved at the same rate. Therefore, we need to change our conscious thoughts to shift from negativity and criticism to positive considerations and feedback.

Let's look at criticism versus feedback. I ran across Figure 12 on the Benedictine University website and the table resonated with the way I think about the two.

Criticism	Feedback
Focuses on what we don't want/don't like	Focuses on what we do want/do like
Is focused on the past	Is focused on the future
Is focused on weaknesses	Is focused on strengths
Deflates	Inspires
Says, "You're the problem."	Says, "We can make this better together."

FIGURE 12

If I could add to this table, I would include that criticism separates; feedback connects.

Anxiety and Feedback

If you're like several people I know, providing feedback can produce anxiety, stemming from a sense of uncertainty, dread, or apprehension. You may feel your heart beating fast, jaw tightening, or stomach cramping. You may notice that your thinking isn't as clear as you'd like, and you may have self-doubts. All of these are normal symptoms of anxiety when giving feedback.

So much has changed in our world over the past several years. We are coming to new awareness around issues of race, class, and gender. All are necessary to positively advance. But as we learn to be better leaders who value diversity, it can sometimes feel like we're all walking on proverbial eggshells, one way or another. People are more anxious about saying the wrong thing, or that their words will be taken out of context, or that we'll blunder and make some social gaffe. Depending on your age and stage of life, and how much training you've received around these important social issues, you may be hyper-cautious about saying anything for fear you'll be viewed as sexist, racist, ageist, or disrespectful. Nobody wants to be shunned, shamed, blamed, and ostracized, and so it's tempting to remain silent. And yet, fear that keeps you from speaking honestly to others is counterproductive, and not just in the workplace.

Devoid of communication, we create environments characterized by isolation and separation that produce poor results and even feelings of despair. There are simple, basic ways to reduce pre-feedback anxiety. I'll start with the basic ones. Prior to providing feedback, it helps to eat healthy foods, get some good rest, and take five to ten deep belly breaths. Make and take the time to think about the person you will be providing feedback to. What do you value about this person? Why is this person important to you? How will this feedback help that person thrive? It will also be helpful to provide yourself with some grace, knowing you are doing the best you can and accepting that everything may not go as perfectly as you'd like.

Being well-informed is another way to calm anxiety, though it requires a little more time and willingness to dig deep. Know something about the person's work history, be aware of their specific set of responsibilities, be clear on what they signed up for and what they are delivering. There are other things too of equal importance, which require sensitivity and self-awareness. Do you know what pronoun the person wants to be known by? Do you understand your own internal bias? How will you protect against it? We don't only need to manage our employees; we need to be willing to look honestly at and manage our own internal proclivities. If something is getting in the way of our offering impartial feedback, then we need to do the work necessary to change that. Knowledge is always going to be a friend of feedback. When you are clear about the person to whom you are offering feedback, and when you understand who you are in their presence, you can have confidence that you are in a good position to effect positive change.

In interviewing people about the topic of feedback and why they are anxious or hesitant to provide feedback, I've come up with the following list for your reference. Notice which ones stand out for you. These will point you toward areas you can work on and learn to manage, as part of your feedback strategy.

Reasons people are typically anxious or hyper-cautious about providing feedback:

- Allowing fear to take precedence over the purpose of the feedback. The fear clouds the purpose.
- Worrying more about yourself versus the impact of your feedback.
- It's harder for a low-level employee to give feedback than a high-level employee because of the fear of being fired or losing their job. Consider creating a culture of safety.
- Breakdown of relationship/loss of relationship after providing feedback.
- Haven't been taught how to provide feedback.
- Frightened of reaction to feedback.
- Don't know what to say.
- Don't have the right words.
- Not sure of the best time.
- Not sure how to begin the conversation.
- Needing to be liked.
- Worried there will be backlash.
- Frightened of saying the wrong thing and getting into trouble.
- Gender issues, race issues, language issues.
- Not sure of intention/purpose/desired outcome.
- The somebody who needs feedback is my boss.
- The somebody who needs feedback is dependent on this job.
- The somebody who needs feedback is intimidating.
- Creating a bad atmosphere at work.
- Not my place.
- Too much on my plate already.
- I shouldn't have to give feedback; isn't it obvious what's wrong?

Social Media and Feedback

Here's what's confusing to me. In a world where there is a deficiency of feedback in the workplace, there is a deluge of it in the realm of social media. It feels like everyone is willing to share anything with anyone for the sake of feedback. It's as if we crave feedback. We're looking for a "like," a "share," a "care," or a "celebration" emoji and won't be satisfied until we get that attention. What's more, if we dare to share anything critical or controversial, we may just end up drowning in a sea of public outrage and critical comments, which is also feedback, but not the welcome or constructive variety. I recall several years ago when a friend of mine provided a viewpoint on social media and another friend responded with feedback that was laced with anger and threats, in this very public, social space. Yet, that person would have never provided that feedback (if any) in a private conversation. What is it about the public nature of social media that creates this bravado around giving feedback online?

What I've come to believe is that social media, because it is a virtual space, psychologically frees us to communicate many of the things that we want to say to someone's face, but don't. We unleash our worst and most judgmental selves without fear of consequence. It's as if social media has become a feedback dumping ground. And to be fair, we are as free in our praise as we are in our criticisms. Social media allows for feedback, unleashed. It has also untethered our ability sometimes to be responsible with how we provide constructive feedback. Social media also offers some other interesting aspects. Unlike face-to-face feedback, it affords the opportunity to process feedback and to reflect on how or if we want to respond. When feedback occurs in person, we tend to believe we need to respond immediately, before we've fully absorbed it.

Over time, social media channels have created a unique platform for posting and sharing our everyday lives for others to comment upon. Through these channels, we've created a culture of influencing others and generating followers, all with the goal of eliciting feedback. I will say, most people turn to social media for positive feedback; however, there are some "trolls" out there who want just any reaction. I also think it's vital we don't replace in-person feedback systems with online ones.

Feedback Is a Version of Truth Telling

Truth-telling is at the core of developing deep connections with others. Of course, choosing when and how to tell the truth depends on several factors. Some truth-telling comes across as overly frank, harsh, or rude. Some comes across as too passive, wishy-washy, or not to the point. Even so, finding your own way of telling the truth in a direct and kind way is critically important to having meaningful and successful relationships.

Don't get me wrong—I've not always been a master of truth-telling. Remember my introduction? I am a reformed pleaser, accommodator, make-better person. I wanted to be nice. I wanted to be liked. I valued others' opinions more than my own—until that version of myself no longer served me. Either as a leader or a person.

Sharing feedback could be considered the same as sharing a perspective. Your perspective. Your observation. Your opinion. Your truth. It doesn't have to be about being right/wrong, good/bad, or win/lose. If we consider ourselves to be on the same team, wanting similar outcomes, why wouldn't we be open to sharing and, when the favor is returned, receiving feedback?

What I'm curious about is how we can create environments in which we all feel comfortable, free from walking on eggshells and/or hesitant to say what's on our mind and in our heart. It would seem that this type of environment could be created if we normalized feedback. Believe me, you may not always get it 100 percent right. But you will be planting seeds and role-modeling for others. Take this story.

—————————————————

I was having some challenges with one of my employees. Her work was "okay" but not what I would call consistent, predictable, or timely. Her general behavior was inconsistent too. We never knew exactly who was going to show up each day. Would we see the positive, helpful person or the negative, resentful person? I generally enjoyed working with and cared for this employee. I wanted her to succeed and needed to let her know how she was both performing and "showing up" for work.

One afternoon prior to her leaving for a week-long vacation, I decided it was time to share my observations.

We sat down in a conference room, and I asked her how things were going for her; what she liked about her work, her co-workers, and the company. I asked her how she thought she was doing in her role. During the conversation, I noticed that she had a defensive posture (arms over chest), and through her short answers, appeared on edge. As she responded to my questions, I caught glimpses of her awareness that she wasn't doing her best work.

I then said, "Here's the thing, you are well-liked and respected here. However, your work product and general behavior at work is unpredictable, inconsistent, and often late. As you are going on vacation for the upcoming week, I would really like you to think about whether you want to work here, with me and the others. I don't believe you are doing your best work. Something must change, and you have ultimate control and choice over what you want and how you will perform. If you don't have all the tools, resources, and support you need, let me know and we'll provide it for you. I want you to be both successful and happy. And, given this discussion and my prior observations, you're not either of those two. When you return, I will want your answer. If your answer is that you choose to be here and are committed to improving in all areas, I'll expect to see it and I'll support you all the way. If your answer is you'd like to move on, I will support helping you find another position that you believe you will be successful and happy in performing. Either way, something must change."

I'm happy to report that that employee returned with the commitment to stay in my department. By giving the employee the choice regarding what she wanted, she was able to freely shift her behavior and attitude toward her work. I could immediately see the impact of her commitment as her performance was better than it ever had been and she seemed genuinely happy. We continued to work together for the next four years.

Nothing Will Change Unless You Do

Mahatma Gandhi's quote, "Be the change you wish to see in the world," resonates for me with the work of giving feedback.

While I've not always been the best at giving feedback, I continue to work on this element of communication for/of myself. I encourage my clients to do the same. I truly believe in and try to live every day through one of Brené Brown's quotes, "Clear is kind." The importance of being clear allows you to cut through inconsequential "stuff" to get to the important "stuff." Being clear and kind means finding and practicing using opening phrases that work for your style. Rather than dancing around saying the thing that needs to be said, consider the following:

- I noticed something in the [name the thing] that I'd like to share with you. Are you open to feedback?
- I know one of your values is [name value]. During an earlier meeting, I noticed something that may not have been in alignment with that value. Are you open to my observation?
- I care about you and want you to succeed. Would you be open to my sharing something that I see could be getting in your way?
- Other clear, concise, and kind phrases could be more firmly stated:

- We agreed that you would be available for work by 8:30 a.m. each morning. I've noticed a pattern of you showing up between 8:45 and 9:00 a.m. It's important that you are here by 8:30 a.m. What's getting in your way in meeting that expectation?
- You committed to having the Q3 plan and details ready for my review by May 15. It's now May 16. What's causing this delay?
- I just observed you speaking rudely to a customer. What was that about? What do I need to know?

As I've explored this topic and put myself "on the court" to practice this skill, I've found that giving feedback from a positive, playful space is a way to connect with others. Especially with those whom we really care about and who carry a fair amount of "armor." These people can seem so controlling, protected, and aggressive that when it comes to giving feedback, it feels like all you want to do is slide an unsigned letter under their office door and then run away as fast as you can. And yet, that seems so inauthentic and weak.

What if you were to take a different approach? Think about Chapter 6: A Unique Way of Thinking About Feedback. What hat would you choose to provide feedback? Finding your way into giving honest feedback that's appropriate to the person and situation is an art, as I've said. So, practice, practice, practice. It is possible to be critical and kind. Indeed, I'd say it was essential.

The Importance of Positive Feedback

Here's another fun fact about feedback. Most feedback that is provided to people is perceived as negative feedback. Why is this? As referenced earlier in this chapter, according to Dr. Rick Hanson the brain is more susceptible to remembering negative experiences or feedback. He mentions that the brain is like Velcro for negative experiences and Teflon for positive experiences.

Most feedback or constructive criticism seminars encourage people to provide balanced feedback, to ensure that the feedback helps to provide development opportunities. When this happens, however, we need to be on high alert for the fact that any perceived negative feedback is going to be experienced and recalled with way more weight than any acknowledgment or praise So if you always provide what you see as "balanced" feedback, be aware that the balance tips in favor of the negative. However, by changing our practices in providing genuine, positive feedback, we can help not only ourselves but also those to whom we offer feedback.

Positive feedback boosts confidence, engagement, and motivation. It propels people into doing their best work. That's why I am choosing to remind us that it's equally, if not more important, to provide frequent positive feedback. Studies on positive psychology remind us of the importance of looking for those things that are going well and meeting expectations, because it helps us to do more of those good things.

Early in my career, my boss and I were asked to work on a compensation project by the chief operating officer of the organization. The project was extremely confidential and complex and had a very tight deadline. Only my boss and I were to know about the details and impacts to various people in the organization. I was both nervous and honored to work on a highly confidential project for this executive. My boss and I worked long hours, ran through several complex calculations and scenarios, and came up with three solutions and a final recommendation just slightly ahead of the deadline. The information was delivered to the executive. From the time we turned in the assignment until we heard back, we were both anxious about how our recommendations would be received. Questions on our minds were, "Did we do it right?

Was it enough data? Did we meet his expectations?" And so forth.

Two days after the executive received the information, he asked us to meet with him in his big corner office. It was the first time I had ever seen his office and I was intimidated. The executive made us more than comfortable, however. With a big smile on his face, he asked us to sit down. He said he had a few questions and a few suggested changes. We listened to his questions and feedback, which all seemed reasonable to us. Toward the end of the meeting, the executive thanked us for our contributions. "What the two of you produced in such a short time and with this level of valuable information is something I haven't experienced from the Human Resources department before. I know it took you a lot of time. In fact, I'm guessing you gave up a few evenings and the weekend to create this result, thinking through every scenario. Thank you for sacrificing your personal time. I couldn't be happier with what you've done. I'm pleased to let you know that for your valuable contribution, you will each receive a bonus in your next paycheck."

We expressed our gratitude, committed to making the few changes he requested, and left his office. The bonus did come, which was nice. What meant more than that, however, was his acknowledgment of our contributions and the value they added to the organization, recognizing that we gave up personal time to produce what he had requested. I learned that that level of affirmation made me want to perform well in every situation. This leader not only provided positive feedback in words and with the bonus, but also the icing on the cake. A bouquet of beautiful flowers was waiting on our desks the following Monday morning. Talk about feeling appreciated!

It's no secret that people generally respond to positive feedback. In fact, one of the wonderful and predictable (at least in my experience) things about positive feedback is that when it's provided in a sincere manner, it inspires people to continue to repeat and occasionally improve upon what they've heard.

Feedback Taboos

- Providing feedback that isn't timely (more than a week after the incident).
- Providing feedback that is vague or is lost in the classic "feedback sandwich" (praise/criticism/praise).
- Providing feedback that is not directly from you or that you haven't personally observed. In other words, putting yourself into the middle of something that you haven't personally experienced.
- Providing feedback that is laced with generalities and lacking specificity.
- Not following up or checking in on the feedback that was provided (just letting it drift off into the distance).
- Reacting to the person's reaction to the feedback. (Remember, people will respond based on what's there for them in that immediate moment. Often it has nothing to do with you.)

Several years ago, I was working with a content designer on creating workbooks that supported my presentation slides. The workbooks were meant to provide a place for people to take notes and capture what they were learning in my leadership development courses. After completing the first workbook, I shared with the content designer that I was delighted with what she created. I could tell that she was both happy and surprised with my response. She asked, "What is it that you like?"

I provided specific and clear feedback. "I really appreciate how you've captured and incorporated both the brand and my 'style' into the workbook. It's easy to read and follow and is aesthetically pleasing. It's clear that you took your time and put thought into the final product. What do you think?"

She said, "Thank you! I really wanted to meet your expectations. This was a fun project. I would like to add something to the workbook. Are you open to my feedback?"

My response was "Absolutely. What are you thinking?"

She said, "Given your audience, I think we could make the workbook a little more 'fun' and less 'corporate-ty.' I found a few funny memes we could incorporate and thought perhaps we could add a page or too for doodling or creative thought. What do you think?"

"Yes, of course! I'd like to see what you envision. Please add your creative thoughts and we can see where we go from there."

The next iteration of the workbook was phenomenal. Her instincts were spot on and improved things significantly.

This interaction also opened the ability to collaborate and create together, and over time, allowed us both to share constructive criticism on other projects we worked on together without any fear.

REFLECTIONS / PRACTICES

Here are a few prompts for you to consider as you prepare to provide positive feedback:

- I want to appreciate you for...
- I couldn't let this moment go by without thanking you for...
- I want you to know exactly why your contributions made such a difference to this...

KEY TAKEAWAY

We all share similar fears and anxieties about giving feedback. But we also have a common path to overcome them.

CHAPTER 9

Ghosting:
A Contemporary Twist on Feedback

The hardest part about being ghosted is the fact you can't deal with the ghoster directly. You just never hear from them again, and everything feels odd and incomplete.

~Mallory Ortberg

An organization I was working with had been without sales leadership for several months. Once they filled the role, they were excited for this new leader, a perfect fit, to start. As the starting day neared, the soon-to-be employee and the CEO had several extensive conversations regarding initial priorities and the long-term vision for the organization. The CEO sent a celebratory gift certificate for a meal to the new candidate and his partner. When the first day came, the new candidate never showed up. Never called. After several weeks of not hearing any word, the recruiter finally reached the sales leader, who only shared, "The position wasn't the right fit after all."

My client and the organization were devastated. To this day, they don't have a concrete explanation for what happened or what triggered the "no show" response. Without concrete feedback provided, they didn't know what adjustments to make for the next hire.

Trends of Ghosting in Organizations

Beginning in 2021, tens of millions of workers left their jobs. This period, referred to as the Great Resignation, the Great Reset, and the Great Awakening, resulted in the resignation of 23.5 percent of the total U.S. workforce. According to Zippia.com, 28 percent of those leaving reported that they had no other work lined up. More often than not, they were leaving without sharing the details of why. Employees simply walked out. This exodus hit companies hard, especially as many were still recovering from the financial blows delivered by the COVID pandemic.

Most of us are familiar with the concept of "ghosting." It occurs when a relationship ends without any communication or reason as to why. One person, or party, simply disappears. You may have experienced some form of ghosting in your personal life, but it's now becoming one of the most disturbing trends gathering steam in the workplace. According to Visier, a People Analytics and Workforce Planning Software Company, of those surveyed about the workplace, 37 percent have ghosted a company and 30 percent have ghosted a potential employer. The reasons given for ghosting are, among others: non-competitive pay practices, more attractive opportunities, and concerns about the company culture. Nor is this a one-way street. Employers are increasingly ghosting employees too, as I will explore later in this chapter.

In early 2022, I was browsing the online question forum, Quora, and came across a question regarding workplace ghosting that really stuck with me. The CEO who posted the question asked whether anyone had heard the term "ghosting" used in relationship to employment. His company had offered a position to someone who had accepted the job, showed up for a day or two, and then was never seen or heard from again. The CEO had learned that his new hires were continuing to interview after accepting a job with his company. Over drinks with colleagues, he also discovered that several of them had recently employed those he had hired and who "ghosted him." Even after accepting an offer, candidates continued looking for newer, better jobs, with a better title, more pay, better benefits, or added flexibility. Once the "better" or "perfect" offer comes in, the employee simply accepts the new offer and fails to notify the previous organization they are leaving. They just disappear. This, the group discovered, was part of a pattern that was impacting all of them.

So how is it that someone feels free to take a job and then just walks away a few days or weeks later, with no explanation? While not illegal, unless you've specifically signed a binding agreement, this practice is considered unethical. After all, a company has paid to recruit you, hire you, and onboard you. When you walk away, the company must start the process all over again, at no small cost of time and money. And while it may feel like a good decision to up and leave for a better job with more status, it's a decision that may haunt your career. You don't want to be known as an employee who has no loyalty or integrity. The world is small, and people talk.

Neither courageous nor honest, ghosting happens when real communication is no longer part and parcel of working life, when the value of real connection, real community, and real conversation has faded into the background, and people feel no obligation to be upfront and truthful about their ambitions or situations. Ghosting is the ultimate symptom of relationship breakdown, and it can play out in various ways within the context of employment, from candidates not showing up for interviews to new hires disappearing into the ether without a word.

Ghosting, in other words, is the result of a system in which the feedback mechanism has broken down. Ghosting can only exist when you think that you don't owe anyone an explanation, or that no one will take seriously your concerns, or that your voice doesn't matter, or that it's nobody's business what you think. This lack of connection or care for others, this sense that whatever you say is useless, reveals a fundamental fracturing of relationships. And the more feedback gets shelved because it's too hard or too embarrassing or time consuming, then the harder and less pleasurable the business of doing business becomes. After all, one of the reasons to work for a company, is for the *company*—the friendship. But if we can walk away without a word, or let someone go without an explanation, camaraderie becomes non-existent.

———

I had a client who hired someone to fill a position, and one month into his employment, the employee called to say he had been in a minor car accident and needed to take the next two days off. My client approved the requested time off, and then never heard from him again. She called the employee and left messages. She called his emergency contact and left a message. She scoured the web for any news and neither received a call back nor learned anything from the news. Nothing. Poof! The employee had vanished without a trace. Now when she hires anyone on her team, my client finds it deeply stressful. She no longer trusts that people are going to stay in their roles. They may simply disappear, leaving her and her team in the lurch.

———

What causes people to leave organizations—or simply never show up—without any words or feedback? I've given a few reasons and we'll look at more. But the question I am struggling with is this: Is it a new human behavior we are normalizing? If so, this is terrible and traumatizing, unsatisfying and unhelpful. Leaving without an explanation of what did/did not work does not allow for change or improvement, and it creates a level of cynicism and skepticism that is not healthy for any person or any organization.

Why Does Ghosting Occur?

Things I hear from interviewees who don't show up or new hires who walk away include:

- I don't owe them anything.
- I don't want to tell them why this other company is more exciting to me.
- I feel embarrassed that I am leaving so soon.
- If I say anything, they'll make it harder for me to leave.

The things that I hear from clients include:
- Don't have to get "into a situation" where I don't know what the outcome will be.
- I can't control what the other person is going to do or say.
- I don't want to hurt anyone's feelings.
- I'm afraid to give feedback.
- I don't want to get into an argument.
- I won't be able to control the situation.
- It takes less energy.
- It's easier to walk away.
- I don't have confidence in how to say something.

Essentially, people are afraid of feeling uncomfortable, getting hurt, or being rejected.

The Impact of Organizations Ghosting Employees

Typically, it is the employee who "walks away" without a word. However, I've been finding more and more situations where leaders and employers are using this tactic as a way out of tough conversations. Take the following story.

After being "ghosted" by his previous workplace, Mat came to me for both career and leadership coaching. I'd heard about ghosting and had even experienced it with a few coaching clients who simply stopped showing up without giving a reason. But I'd never heard about an incident of ghosting like Mat's.

Over the course of five years, Mat had successfully taken his team from three to sixty-five employees, with very little turnover. They had achieved their performance goals sixteen out of twenty quarters and continued to meet the rising demands of the organization. The overall team performance was solid. There were, according to his manager, a few of Mat's leadership skills such as improved communication, accountability and feedback that needed development. Mat took this feedback seriously. He read books on leadership, responded to his boss's requests, and did what he knew to do to achieve the results being asked of him. He also focused on continuing to build and develop his team.

After Mat had been with the organization several years, a new leadership development workshop was introduced. Mat, along with eight of his peers, were told to attend a twelve-week training. Mat described the training to me as rudimentary, and after the first three sessions he didn't see the value of attending any longer. He missed the next session, without notifying the course facilitator. However, he had explained the situation to his manager, who had supported his decision to discontinue. So, Mat continued to miss the sessions. About halfway through the program, the facilitator of the leadership development series, who had great influence with the CEO, contacted Mat. Mat described the facilitator as aggressive and condescending. He told Mat that there was no choice about whether to attend the sessions. He was expected to be there. Mat responded that the training was like one he had attended twenty years prior and this one wasn't providing value.

When Mat told his manager about the confrontation, his manager told him not to worry and to stay focused on his job. He needed Mat to focus on obtaining sales results. He would take care of the situation.

One day, and without explanation, Mat was demoted. Overnight, all invites to leadership-related meetings were canceled. Mat met with his manager and the CEO about his demotion. Their response was limited to, "This is the right thing for the organization at this time." Mat asked for specific reasons for being demoted but wasn't told why. The meeting lasted all of three minutes. Lacking information, Mat told me that the only story that made sense to him is that the facilitator of the leadership training had spoken with the CEO about him, and this had resulted in his demotion. Mat continued with the organization for almost three months. He received no contact or communication from his boss or the CEO, or anyone else in the organization. Meetings were declined. Emails were ignored. His direct reports didn't show up for meetings he scheduled. It was almost like he wasn't there. He had been ghosted. He reached out to HR several times, indicating that none of this made sense and wanted an explanation. Finally, the HR person met with him and presented him with a one-year separation package indicating that his role was being eliminated. Still, he received no explanation from HR and no communication from his manager, the CEO, or anyone who had previously been on his team.

The experience was so devastating that in addition to career coaching with me, Mat began undergoing therapy. He was left angry, hurt, confused, and in a place where he felt he could not trust another employer again.

You, like me, may be shaking your head and saying, "Can this really be true?" Could an organization be so callous as to cut off a valuable employee of many years, without explanation? The answer, unfortunately, is yes. But Mat's story has another component to it, which is this: Your employees deserve to know exactly what is required of them. If it was mandatory for Mat to attend those meetings, then his manager and CEO owed it to Mat to make that clear. So, the first sin of omission was not telling Mat that if he didn't attend, he would face repercussions. Then, to ghost him for a behavior that they helped to create by not communicating clearly is simply adding insult to injury. And while I can't speak for the company, I hope they recognize the negative impact they had on Mat's life and career. Others in the organization probably suffered from what happened to Mat too. People in these types of organizations operate with a "heads down" approach, hoping to avoid being the next target. Most likely, that's one of the reasons no one came to Mat's defense.

The Impact of Organizations Ghosting Candidates

My colleague Jan applied for a position with a large Fortune 500 company and was fortunate to go all the way through the interview process, starting with the recruiter, then the hiring manager, and finally with the head of the department. She even met with the team she would be leading. The role required her to relocate. She visited the city that might become her new home and talked at length with the hiring manager about the best areas to live, and how long it might take to get situated, should she get the job. As one of two top candidates for the role, Jan was told she would hear a definitive answer soon. Several days passed and Jan never heard back from anyone. She reached out to the recruiter and the hiring manager but heard nothing back. She even tried to connect with some of the team members through LinkedIn. Again, she heard nothing. After two months, she stopped trying. Jan was confused by the entire process. The hiring manager's encouragement to check out places to live was so validating. To hear nothing back was devastating. And, as Jan described, it was also disrespectful and unkind. Jan's impression of the company and the people she met plummeted. Jan has openly shared her negative experience with others in her networks, which reflects badly on the organization and will only make it harder for them to recruit top talent.

———————————

Let's agree here, that after making it through many milestones in the recruitment process, having invested her time and energy to engage in and get excited about the opportunity, the very least Jan deserved was a phone call from the hiring manager explaining why they chose another candidate. Receiving this feedback might have helped in her next career transition. But more than that, the feedback would have provided Jan with closure, and a better experience with the organization.

The Consequences of Ghosting

When leaders do not say what needs to be said, they perpetuate a "closed" or non-communicative culture. This type of organizational or leadership behavior can add to employees quietly quitting or suffering silently until they resign, without explanation.

Until a culture of feedback is woven into an organization, it is inevitable that the absence of feedback, to the point of ghosting, is not going to go away. Normalizing ghosting doesn't eliminate the distress or trauma of being ghosted. When someone has been ghosted more than once, as reported in the article "The 7 Essential Psychological Truths about Ghosting" by Loren Soeiro, Ph.D., ABPP, a weird sense of apathy or normalization occurs. At the same time, ghosting creates confusion and a void in the person's life. These two competing ideas create cognitive dissonance. For some, it inflicts a psychological wound that erodes trust and a sense of human-to-human connection.

Increased usage of dating apps, Zoom meetings, and other technologies encourages the upturn in ghosting. It's easier to walk away from a person you only meet with online. And because it's happening more and more, we might feel, "That's okay. I kind of expected to be ghosted (or this to happen)." Below the surface, however, this experience may lead to an internalized sense of self-doubt, self-criticism, or loss of confidence. Over time, these types of thoughts or feelings may hinder our ability to be vulnerable and to trust, both key components in the development of intimate relationships in life and work. This results in us bringing less of ourselves to our job performances and professional relationships. This lack of investment in our energy and care doesn't just impact the company culture, but the bottom line.

The Consequence of Ghosting Consultants, Vendors, or Partners

Over a six-month period, I consulted as an interim HR executive with an organization, providing change management and leadership development. As often happens, within a few weeks, my responsibilities expanded to include other organizational needs. Soon I was considered part of the executive team providing HR strategy, leadership, coaching, and overseeing HR tasks provided by an outside vendor.

It was clear the organization needed a full-time HR leader, and, at the time, I wasn't interested in the role. I recommended that an executive recruiting firm be engaged to interview prospects and that I remain involved in the process. Based on my experiences with the company, I could provide an essential perspective on organizational needs and culture fit. Despite my offer, however, I wasn't consulted or involved in the hiring process. I chose to respect their decision.

Fortunately for the organization, they were able to find a qualified HR candidate. They told me the hire date of the new leader and, at the same time, notified me that my engagement would end within two weeks. I asked what I could do to prepare the organization for the change and the hand-off from me to the new HR leader. In my professional experience, it is standard protocol to provide a warm welcome to any successor and to aid the transition. But my offer was again turned down. I left the office one afternoon, a week before my contract expiration date. That evening, I signed on to my computer to finalize a few tasks. I noticed my access to several tools was cut off.

I first contacted the IT department and was told to talk to the CEO. I called the CEO, and my call went to voicemail.

The next morning, I arrived at the office and my security badge was disabled. I again contacted the CEO and when my call went to voicemail, I contacted the CTO. He said that his team was just complying with the request from the CEO, which was to cut off all access. While I understood the protocol, I had a few things yet to complete that had been agreed upon between the CEO and me. And yet here I was, standing outside a locked building, unable to fulfill those commitments. My integrity felt out of sorts. I couldn't understand why I was shut out without any explanation.

A few days later, I received a call from the company's sales manager, who asked me for some employee relations guidance. I was confused by the call after being "cut off" the prior week, but responded, "Thanks for calling me; however, you should work this through with the new HR leader."

He said, "What? What new HR leader?"

While I thought, "This is awkward. Have they not announced my departure and the new HR leader's arrival?" I said, "Let me help you with this immediate issue. I'll see if I can provide you with the information for the new HR leader so you can go to that person the next time you have a question." I guided him through the situation and upon completing our call, I called the CEO. Again, it went to voicemail. I left the CEO a respectful but direct message that he needed to communicate with the organization about the leadership transition. I notified him I was still being contacted for guidance when I was no longer working for the company. In my message, I stated that the lack of change management and communications was confusing to me, and I imagined his organization.

A few months after my departure, I received a phone call from the CTO. He sounded apologetic. "I'm sorry that I couldn't say much about what was happening when your access was 'cut off.' I want to tell you this: You were valued by everyone in the organization." He paused for a moment, then continued, "In my entire career, I've never been involved with treating a transition like this in such a bizarre manner. Especially with a key leadership position."

He went on to explain, "When you left, it was like you were never here. As if those six months consulting with us had never happened. There was no explanation about why your contract ended. There was no big announcement about the new leader. One day you were here and the next day we had a new HR leader. It was as though a magic switch had been thrown. It's been a tough transition for the new HR leader too. I just wanted to let you know."

I thanked the CTO and hung up the phone. Since leaving that organization, I had felt a sense of loss. Like I was part of something, but maybe wasn't. It was confusing. I had literally been cut off, in the worst and most disrespectful manner. As though I had never existed or contributed. The aftermath I was left with was one of mistrust and anger, which even the CTO's call couldn't banish. What's more, the reputation of the organization I had once held in high regard was now completely eroded. Even today, it's not an organization I would recommend to a vendor, partner, potential employee, or customer. The way they dealt with a relatively easy transition ended up being unnecessarily messy and confusing.

FUN FACT ABOUT GHOSTING

When did the term *ghosting* become mainstream?

The term *ghosting* became popular and more widely used with the advent of online dating. These platforms allowed people to make themselves "invisible" after connecting with someone online. Merriam-Webster made *ghosting* an official entry in the dictionary in 2017.

What It Looks Like to NOT Ghost
(Accepting Responsibility)

I am on the board of directors for a local HR executive association. Several of us partner together on program design and speaker selection. We also rely heavily on volunteers to provide their time and expertise so that we can grow the association and create successful professional development and networking opportunities.

———————————

A year ago, Cate joined our organization and expressed interest in helping us with our programming needs. Like many other volunteers, Cate had a highly visible role in her community, volunteered with other associations, and had the additional responsibility of running her business. Cate recently contacted me to let me know that she needed to resign her role with the programming committee and would not be renewing her membership with our organization. She was direct, clear, and kind. Cate shared that she had several personal things occurring in the upcoming year and she wanted to be 100 percent present for these important moments. She had a son graduating from college and another one getting married. She said, "I know I could power through and do all the things required of me, but I want to be most present with these precious life moments. I do not want to be distracted with thoughts or things that are going to take away from these memories. Therefore, I needed to let you know as soon as I knew."

I thanked Cate for her courage and authenticity in sharing this information with me. She said, "I respect you and others in the association, Joni. Sharing this information was important to me and for our ongoing relationship. When I see you in public, I don't want to avert my eyes because I did not share my truth. More importantly, when this is over, I want to have the opportunity to come back to the association and be welcomed with open arms.

When I think about Cate and her choice to be transparent, I see her as a role model to others on the importance of being upfront about their circumstances. I wish more people were able to behave this way. Especially when it comes to providing meaningful feedback on why a person is not fit for a role or why a role is not the right fit for a person at that present time.

The Importance of Creating a Culture of Connection

One day I asked a client's employee, "What is challenging about working here?"

The employee paused, looked down, and said, "I ask my manager a specific question and my manager promises to get back to me with an answer by a certain date. And then, I never hear back from my manager. Two to three weeks pass. I ask my manager the same question and get the same answer. At this point, my manager barely looks at me in team meetings and cancels our one-on-one meeting with an excuse of 'being too busy.'"

As I reflected on this employee's answer, my mind played back to several other similar stories I had heard throughout my career. Whether an employee asks for a raise, career mapping, or a promotion, the manager often isn't armed with the tools or support to respond to the employee in a timely or confident manner. Thus, the manager instead chooses not to directly answer the question, and the employee/manager relationship begins to fracture.

A role I play with organizational clients is to interview employees to identify themes of engagement or disengagement. The purpose is to uncover pain points that employees don't bring up to their manager(s). When I capture the information, I present it in an anonymous and consolidated format to remove emphasis from who is providing a perspective, and instead to focus on how often a certain topic or pain point comes up. To ensure a trusting relationship with employees during these interviews, and because I often find that people are hesitant to share feedback, I speak directly about the confidentiality of their responses. Employees either don't think their voices matter or they don't trust the information will be handled in a professional manner. In all the years of conducting these interviews, the leader who hires me honors my commitment to keep responses confidential. If this assurance was breached, my reputation and credibility would be tarnished, and the connection between the organization's leader and their employees would break down.

A common theme employees express if they haven't experienced a culture of feedback is the perception that no one cares anyway. I've learned that if feedback isn't given to employees on a regular basis, the relationship and connection between manager and employee is held together by a "thread," if at all. It's no wonder that employees walk away without saying anything. It takes less energy. It's certainly avoiding conflict. And, as the story goes, "my feedback won't matter anyway." If they have been led to believe that no one cares enough to ask their opinion, or to offer constructive feedback, why would anyone care if they walked away?

THOUGHTS ON FEEDBACK

Sometimes giving no feedback is feedback.

Some people are comfortable with just walking away and not giving feedback. While walking away may consume less energy, it either tells people that you don't value them and the relationship or that you don't believe your voice or opinions are important.

Ghosting is a real phenomenon in our lives today. If we don't normalize feedback, we perpetuate the possibility of ghosting. As leaders and influencers, it is our choice and responsibility in regard to how we want to shape our organizational cultures and the world at large. By standing up and sharing our truth through feedback, we are role-modeling for others how we can provide closure and completion in a respectful and connected way, and we are providing the other with feedback that could potentially be of lifelong value to them.

As captured in this chapter, some people believe that avoiding direct feedback is, in fact, an adequate way of communicating something important. Some believe that walking away or not returning phone calls is enough to show the other person, "I'm done with you." This may be an easier ending for the "giver" of feedback, though it often causes harm to the person on the receiving end. While it's not your personal responsibility to make people feel good, I would leave you with this statement that Brené Brown brought to the world: Being clear is kind. From my perspective, providing closure is kind. It is also morally the right thing to do.

REFLECTION

Think back over your life: Have you ever "ghosted" anyone intentionally or unintentionally before?

- What did you do?
- Why did you do it?
- How did you do it?
- What do you know now?
- What needs to be "cleaned up" to create closure?
- What will you do with the information you now have?

PRACTICE

Often, writing a letter to a person is a good way to practice saying what needs to be said. Notice I said "writing a letter" and not "sending a letter." There's a difference. Writing a letter gives you time and space to think about what you would say to someone, even if you don't send it. It's about practicing and building muscles to say what is truly in your mind and heart.

Think about personal or professional relationships in your life today. Is there someone you haven't been upfront or honest with?

- Who is the person? (Write down their name)
- Who is the person to you, i.e., family member, friend, colleague, employee, spiritual leader? (write that down too)
- Start with an opening sentence or phrase such as:
  - » *I don't know how to say this and...*
  - » *I've been wanting to tell you something...*
  - » *I haven't been completely honest because...*
  - » *There's something you need to know...*
- *Share what's there for you. What is hard to say and why? Here are a few examples:*
  - » *There was a circumstance where I felt...*
  - » *We've been friends for a while, and I've come to realize that...*
  - » *You had been a fantastic employee and I'm noticing that you aren't now. Here's what I've noticed and haven't told you...*
- *Share what you want and why. Here are a few examples:*
  - » *(If a relationship you want to continue) I want to be heard in our relationship. It's important to me because...*
  - » *(If a relationship you don't want to continue) I don't want to see you/be friends/have you employed here anymore because...*

- » *(If an area of someone you work with or who reports to you) I want you to do what I am requesting you do at work. Avoiding accountability to my requests is not acceptable.*
- Close the letter with a salutation that is aligned with what you said, how you felt, and how you would like to leave the person feeling.
  - » *You're important to me and I wanted you to know how I felt.*
  - » *I respect you and wish you the best in the future.*
  - » *I'm grateful to know you and appreciate your consideration.*

After writing the letter, set it aside for a day or two.

In a notebook, calendar, or journal, write how you feel now.

When you bring it back out and review it, is there anything you would change? Is this something you can say to the person? Is it something you will send to the person? What will you do now and why?

KEY TAKEAWAY

Avoiding communication or ghosting is unprofessional and damaging to people and organizations.

CHAPTER 10

Being on the Receiving End of Feedback

Criticism, like rain, should be gentle enough to nourish
a man's growth without destroying his roots.

~Frank A. Clark

Over dinner one night, I shared with friends that I was writing a book about how to give feedback. One of them immediately exclaimed, "Giving feedback is easy! You should teach people how to receive feedback! That's hardest of all. We're all terrible at receiving feedback." This was such great feedback; I've decided to dedicate a chapter to that topic.

If some part of you is wondering, "But why do I have to learn how to receive feedback if this book is about how to provide it?" let me be clear. Every leader needs to have walked the path they are asking their employees to follow them down. We can't expect to create a culture of feedback until we ourselves have become open to receiving it. The truth is, if you don't allow others to give you feedback, you'll never develop the sensitivity and intentionality needed to become great at it. Learning how you respond to feedback, both the flattering and challenging kind, allows you to develop the necessary empathy and awareness to offer impactful feedback. So, let's jump in.

To create context for this chapter around receiving feedback as a leader, I would like to bring back the model from Chapter 5 of this book and the authors of the 15 *Commitments of Conscious Leadership*.

Take a moment and ask yourself: When receiving feedback, are you the person who naturally listens to feedback above the line? Or below the line?

If we think giving feedback is hard, being on the receiving end of it can be so much harder. There's a lot of vulnerability packed around receiving feedback. It just feels so personal. And it is. But its intent is to help us grow, develop, and stretch.

If your internal mindset is "above the line" and you feel secure, curious, and confident, your response to feedback will lean more positive. For example, *"Thank you for sharing that helpful feedback. I hadn't thought about this aspect and what you'd like to see differently. How would you suggest I handle that in the future? Any coaching or advice on how to do that better?"*

Conversely, if your internal mindset is "below the line" and you don't feel safe or are insecure and defensive, your thoughts and belief systems will interpret the feedback as an attack. If you go into a conversation feeling under attack, resentful, or defensive, you will listen and respond through an unconscious filter, filling in the narrative before allowing the actual feedback to "land." In cases like these, it's easy to misinterpret the actual feedback or make stories up about it. "Below the line" thinking often results in these types of responses: *"I knew that anything I produced wasn't going to be good enough. Why can't I ever get it right? I wonder if I am going to be fired. I should look for a new job. Everyone always criticizes my work. They don't appreciate anything I do and I'm sick of working this hard to always hear what I am doing wrong and never feeling appreciated..."*

It is important to "check in" on your mindset when receiving feedback. Additionally, in thinking about feedback you've received in the past, what do you know about your natural reaction? Or are you like most and it "depends on the day or the moment?" Or, who is offering the feedback and how it is being delivered.

Depending on your internal mindset, you might find yourself in one of two places. Growth mindset vs. the fixed mindset which was introduced in chapter 8 on leadership. The concept of growth mindset and fixed mindset was coined by Carol Dweck in her 2006 book on *Mindset: The New Psychology of Success.* In chapter 8, we looked at it from the perspective of the giver of feedback. Now we're going to look at it again, only this time from the receiver's perspective.

Receiver of Feedback

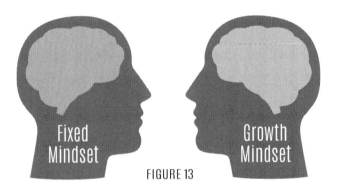

FIGURE 13

When in an open, curious, and growth mindset, feedback can feel really good. We can feel seen, valued, and recognized. We realize we are important enough for someone to take the time to help us do better. As I've said, people want feedback, even if they are fearful of it. To put yourself in a Growth Mindset, consider the following reinforcing responses:

Fixed Mindset = Criticism	Growth Mindset = Feedback
This person is picking on me.	This person cares about me and is trying to help me.
This person thinks I'm bad at this.	This person must believe in me, or s/he wouldn't bother pointing out how I can improve.
I am so angry. I feel so embarrassed.	I'm thankful this person is telling me how I can do this better.
I give up. I'll never be able to do this as well as this person wants me to.	I will try to do the things this person is suggesting and see if it helps me to improve.
This person is out to get me.	This person would like to support my growth and can see something I can't.

FIGURE 14

- Express gratitude to the person providing you with feedback.
- Let the person know if their feedback was meaningful for you and why. Or how the feedback could have been more impactful.
- Reflect on and learn more about what the person is saying. Ask more questions of the person.

If you find that you are in an emotional rut (exasperated, frustrated, wounded, with lots of baggage), you won't see the person for who they are. Use some of the ideas you learned earlier in the book such as:

- Take five to ten deep abdominal breaths.
- Take a quiet walk outdoors, observing what's around you before you respond.
- Consider what is true about the feedback.
- Have you heard this feedback before or is it new?
- If you want to respond to the feedback, take a quick run or dance to music to shift your energetic response.

THOUGHTS ON FEEDBACK

Feedback is ALWAYS Around Us

Every time we speak with a friend, family member, customer, employee, manager, or partner, feedback is laced throughout. At your local coffee shop each morning, even simple things like "Thank you, that was fast!" or "Thank you for noticing my hat!" is feedback.

REFLECTION

Taking what you just learned about growth versus fixed mindset, I invite you to take a few moments and recall some recent feedback you received:

- What do you remember about the situation?
- Who provided the feedback and what is your relationship with that person?
- What was the environment like?
- What was your mindset?
- How did you react?
- Was there a trigger?
  - » If so, what was it?
  - » Take five to ten deep breaths.
  - » Think about the relationship you have/want to have with the feedback giver.
  - » Identify the outcome you'd like to occur next.
- Was the feedback valuable?
- What did you learn?

I recently received feedback from a vendor/partner I've worked with. I share this example as one where I got "triggered" because I was in a "wounded" mindset. While not pretty, I wanted to tell you my story to acknowledge that we all go through experiences like these.

I had worked with a vendor/partner for about five years. This vendor was key in my marketing strategy. From my perspective, our relationship was intact. We respected one another as businesswomen and we were friends, so we knew one another well. She provided me with guidance on several things related to the marketing side of my business. In reviewing my financial reports, I noticed that my investment in marketing wasn't producing the return on investment (ROI) I expected. We had been moving rapidly to make certain changes to my website such as adding an Events tab and refreshing the content. I also mentioned I was interested in getting more into the social media aspects of marketing my business.

While I was thinking about social media, my vendor was talking about creating an SEO strategy. Both are important and both would require more time and money. At a certain point, I felt pressured by this vendor to decide on the next steps. I knew I didn't have the time and I wasn't interested in spending more money. My body instinctively felt like I needed to "pump the brakes" on the project. Rather than rolling with the pressure (which I often did), I chose to take a pause to step back and reflect on what was important to me and my business.

When told by my vendor that I was going to "pause" before making a decision, I received a two-page, single-spaced email of things that we'd been working on together for the past six months. She shared her perspectives and feedback on the project, which I valued and appreciated. However, as I closed in on the end of the email, these words jumped off the page at me: "IF YOU WERE SMART, and like I've been TELLING you for a LONG time, you should blah, blah, blah...." Bingo. Trigger wire tripped. I got defensive fast. No growth mindset for me. I was reactive, defensive, and closed-minded.

Even just reliving this to share it with you makes my heart beat rapidly and my body warm up: "If you were smart." Nice.

———————————

Let me deconstruct this a bit from my own internal state using the reflection I provided earlier in this chapter and specifically focus on the facts:

- **What do you recall about the situation?** *I was working on a project with a vendor.*
- **Who provided the feedback and what is your relationship with that person?** *Someone I have worked with and trusted for the past five years.*
- **What was the environment like?** *Safe. I was in my office while reading the email.*
- **What was your mindset?** *Prior to receiving the email, my mindset was open and curious and I felt great about choosing to pause and reflect on what I really wanted next. After receiving and reading the email, my mindset was closed and defensive.*
- **How did you react?** *I stopped reading the email, pushed away from my desk, and stood up and started pacing. I picked up my phone and set it down several times. I was ticked off and wanted to call her to tell her off.*
- **Was there a trigger?** *I was hurt and triggered by the "If you were smart" comment. This brought up the narrative that I wasn't smart enough (or as smart as her) and that I didn't know what I was doing.*

» Take five to ten deep breaths. *I did that and started to calm down.*

» Identify what kind of relationship you want to have with the person. *I spent time reflecting over the past five years and our relationship from the beginning. What I wanted was a relationship that was collaborative, open, respectful, and trusting. I didn't want to feel pushed or pressured. I wanted a partnership. I contacted the vendor to discuss the situation, her email and intention, and my experience. I suggested that we explore what kind of relationship we wanted to have going forward.*

» What is the outcome you desire? *I really wanted to have a shared common vision with my vendor where we could reset expectations. I also realized after doing some soul searching that I wanted to direct this part of my business versus being told what to do.*

    ▪ *I suggested that we take a micro-break and define what a partnership would look like going forward.*

    ▪ *My vendor suggested we end the work relationship because she didn't want to work with someone who didn't want to value her more than thirty years of experience. She wanted to partner with someone who would do what she told them to do.*

    ▪ *As I thought more about the partnership and what she wanted me to do, I realized that it wasn't a relationship that I wanted. I would like a partnership where input/feedback/curiosity is at play. I'm not good at being told what to do, anyway.*

- **Was the feedback valuable?** *Yes. Upon reflection, the feedback was very valuable:*
  - » *It validated areas I could develop as a business owner.*
  - » *It was a reminder to me that my vendor had been cap-turing what I previously wanted and was expressing frustration that I had changed my mind. I learned when I changed my mind it was impacting her time and focus. Great reminder for me that decisions I make with my business have an impact on those who work with me.*
  - » *It helped me see clearly who I want to partner and work with in the future.*
- **What did you learn?** *That it's good to "ride the wave," so to speak, when reacting to feedback. It's important to notice when you are below the line and to work back up to being curious and open. What I especially appreciate during these experiences is to not "shut down" and to listen to the negative internal saboteurs that might lurk inside.*

Receiving Feedback

I understand when receiving critical feedback that one would be triggered; however, it's fascinating to me that when people receive positive feedback, it can be equally as hard to accept.

I have one client who wants to be valued for her the role she plays in her organization. She wants appreciation and affirmation for her good work and contributions. She often complains that she never receives any real positive feedback and wonders if her boss knows all that she is contributing to the organization. We've spent several sessions working through her internal "critical saboteur" and have been working toward building her sense of self-worth and self-regard.

One day prior to a coaching session, I observed her boss saying to her, "I really value how you are leading your team and the results you are gaining because of your leadership style. Thank you for making a difference." To which she replied as she swept her arm away, "Oh, it's no big deal. It's why you pay me the big bucks, right?" And she laughed while walking away.

When we arrived in her office, I said, "That was a nice compliment that I observed." She said, "Oh that? He doesn't mean it. He's just saying it."

I was stunned. Internally, I was thinking, "Really?" Externally I said, "What exactly do you mean?"

She laughed and said, "I don't believe him. I'm not that good."

Immediately I realized what loop she was in. My client was receiving feedback that she was valuable; however, she was brushing it aside and not believing it because her internal critical saboteur wouldn't allow her to hear and "soak in" the positive feedback.

I asked her to consider that she was that good; however, she had a reflex to brush aside any positive feedback because her internal self-worth wouldn't let her hear it. Immediately my client teared up and said, "I've always reacted that way."

We spent the rest of the session unpacking her natural tendency to brush off positive feedback. We ended the session with this challenge:

Whenever you hear positive feedback, stop, take a deep breath in, exhale, and then say, "Thank you. I appreciate your feedback."

A few weeks later, I received a call from my client saying that she really valued the fact that I observed the exchange between her and her boss. The coaching that followed changed her perspective and she finally felt valued by the organization.

Constructive criticism or critical feedback can also challenge us, but in a different way. When on the receiving end of this type of feedback, I suggest that if you can, you respond in an open, curious, and growth mindset (above the line), to process and engage with the giver of feedback. However, if you feel uneasy, defensive, or triggered (below the line), before you respond to what you've just heard, thank the person, and ask if you can take a minimum of 30 minutes to process (longer if needed).

During the thirty minutes, I would recommend that you first take time to breathe (five to ten deep breaths). It has been proven that when in a stress response, deep abdominal breathing helps to control the nervous system and encourages the body to relax. In doing so, we begin to relax, feel calm, and become open. If it helps to take a walk outside to clear your mind, do that. Studies show that walking outside can also bring us into a more relaxed and open state. By doing either or both things, you may find your way into a place of curiosity about the feedback. You may better understand the motivations of the person who provided it and what you want to do about what was shared with you. If you're still having a hard time putting yourself in a responsive mindset rather than a reactive one, consider the following questions to help get your brain past your emotional reaction. Once you're here, consider the following questions to explore what shows up for you.

- Are you **Open** to what you just heard?
- Are you **Curious** about what you are learning?
- What is your **Connection** to the person who provided the feedback?
- What do you notice about how you are **Breathing**?
- How do you **Process** feedback?
- What **Judgment** or **Criticism** is showing up for you?
- What **Triggers** show up when you heard the feedback?
- Where can you find **Gratitude** in the feedback?
- What have you **Learned** from the feedback?

- **What's next** for you now?

I encourage people to consider and examine their immediate responses. I want them to explore how those responses are serving their personal and professional growth and development, and how it's cultivating their relationships.

Reflections / Practices

I'd like to encourage you to "get on the court" and practice receiving feedback using the exercise described below, which I have personally used and encourage my clients to use. I'm not certain of the original genesis; however, I was introduced to this practice by a colleague, Lynne Williams. The essence of the exercise is to get comfortable with asking for and receiving feedback as a curious observer, without taking it personally.

When we attempt to perceive ourselves as others see us, a whole new world opens, allowing us both access to our blind spots and to greater areas for development and growth. The purpose of the interviews that follow is to let yourself experience how you are seen by the people around you. Looking at yourself through others' eyes can feel vulnerable. I would encourage you to start this exercise with those you feel safe with—friends, family members, and trusted colleagues. Start by interviewing five to seven people to see if you can identify and explore any common themes.

During the interview, your job is to ask the question, listen, and write down exactly what the person says, leaving your own interpretations out of the answer. Do not add, subtract, change, or rephrase. Just write it as they express it. Once the question has been answered and you've captured the exact answer, say, "Thank you. Is there anything else?" This allows your interviewee to hear your gratitude and thus feel safe to go on and say all that needs to be shared.

Follow this same process for all of the questions you ask.

I've provided what I consider to be the first simple, yet essential questions:

1. What are my strengths?
2. What are my weaknesses?
3. What does everyone know about me?
4. What can you always count on me for?
5. What can you never count on me for?

When you've asked all the questions, thank the person who provided you with feedback.

Once you've conducted all the interviews, compile the results, then explore what themes emerge. What have you learned about yourself based on the perceptions that people have shared with you? Consider that nothing is good or bad, or right or wrong. Just be curious. Are you familiar with some of the responses? What is new? What is surprising? What makes you cringe? What themes are you seeing? As you absorb the information, is there anything you'd like to shift in how you are being with others? Only you can decide what you want to do with the information.

As I close this chapter, I want to share my own experience. I've done this exercise several times over the past several years and continue to learn how I come across to others. This information always helps me to transform as a professional and on a personal level.

———————

The first time I did this exercise I learned several things. I'm sharing the top themes with you here:

- *I often put everyone else's needs before my own.*
- *I would do anything for anyone.*
- *People know my family is very important to me.*

- *I don't take time for myself.*
- *I don't return phone calls right away.*
- *People sometimes take advantage of me and I'm treated like a doormat (that made me cringe).*
- *And from my family: Sometimes I put work and our friends in front of not only me, but them too.*

Based on what I learned, I found myself shifting toward putting my needs above others and taking time for myself and to be more present for my family. This helped me set boundaries and removed the "doormat" aspect from my life. Who wants to be treated like a doormat? Not me!

Getting feedback from others may feel hard; however, by leveraging a growth mindset, there is so much value and growth to experience with feedback. What's more, as I said earlier, you can't provide for others what you haven't experienced for yourself.

KEY TAKEAWAY

Receiving feedback, whether positive or negative, helps us to grow as leaders and increases our ability to compassionately provide feedback for others.

CHAPTER 11

Giving Yourself Permission to Offer Feedback

Every ending is a new beginning.

~Marianne Williamson

I started this book as a passion project to explore feedback, when Marc, someone I respect very much, was courageous enough to provide me with the right feedback at the right time.

I will forever be grateful for that feedback for two reasons. One, it uncovered an unconscious behavior and reflex—my people-pleasing saboteur—that I relied on too often and wasn't beneficial to me or others. This opened a door that provided me with the conscious ability and desire to shift that behavior. And two, the feedback increased my awareness of the power of providing feedback in a safe and compassionate manner. I want to share this gift with everyone, every day, and for the right reasons.

Don't get me wrong. Sometimes when we provide feedback to someone we deeply care about, they aren't ready for the feedback. And it may not turn out favorably. While I long for feedback to create deeper, connecting relationships, I also know that the opposite can happen, especially if the feedback isn't given effectively and/or the recipient isn't ready for it.

But feedback, as you know by now, matters. So, I invite you to imagine a world where there is a safe place for all of us to go to practice giving and receiving feedback. In your mind's eye conjure up a white tent, 50 feet tall and 100 feet wide. As you enter the tent you immediately notice how spacious it is and how colorful. There are beautiful pillows and cushions placed here and there to sit on and comfortable places for people to stand and gather. A big sign on the entryway reads: judgey judgertons (as my husband calls them) and shaming shamertons, or blaming blamertons, are not welcome here. Fear, as well, is to be left outside.

When you step into the tent, notice how it feels alive, inviting, comfortable, peaceful, and joyful. There is a sense of familiarity, connectedness, and playfulness all around. People are gathered to practice giving feedback to one another without trepidation. This is a place where people intentionally come to experiment and learn about themselves. A sense of curiosity and confidence prevails, and the feedback sessions uplift everyone in the room. Each person is learning more about themselves, the potential within others, the talents, and the skills to be developed, as well as the shortcomings and areas in need of growth. And it's all okay.

This is my dream of what a culture of feedback can look like. To me, it's one of the most extraordinary and empowering visions we can have as leaders—to create this kind of space for learning, growing, and, together, getting better at what we do. Here's what I know: It's up to each of us as individuals and leaders to care enough about the person in front of us to have the courage to say what we see. Sometimes we may not get it right. And guess what? We just might. We don't know unless we try. And, if we don't try, we will never know.

Feedback is rarely talked about as part of fulfilling our life purpose;

however, when we are disappointed with outcomes, whether professional or personal, it's often because we didn't give clear and concise feedback about what we desired, needed, or felt was important to us. Simply put, we get more out of life and what we want when we ask for it.

I believe that we are all here on this earth to live out our true purpose and to make an impact on the world in some way. If we are intentional in our lives, we will be better equipped to realize our own potential and help others to realize theirs. If you are the person who can give and receive feedback through a curious, compassionate, and growth mindset, relationships will develop, blossom, and grow. And the world, or at least your corner of it, will be a better place for all to live. I hope that throughout this book, you've been engaging in the practices and have begun to develop your own style, competencies, and confidence in providing feedback. While I write this conclusion, I am acutely aware that it's just the beginning. It's the beginning for you and others in your life to start a new practice in creating caring, connected relationships through giving meaningful, heartfelt feedback to the right person, in the right way, at the right time.

I wish you all the very best as your journey with feedback continues.

KEY TAKEAWAY

If we ALL considered feedback with an air of openness and possibility, we would free us all up to do our best work and live true to our purpose.

Additional Feedback Tools

Ninety Day Check-In Interview

Used by an employee's leaders or Human Resources to initiate a conversation and exploration on how things are going with the new employee after ninety days. Provides feedback and insights on what's going well and what can be changed to ensure the employee is doing the job they were hired for and they are having a great experience at work.

You've been with [name of company] for over ninety days. The purpose of this conversation is to check in and see how things are going.

- Overall impression after working with [Company] after ninety days.
- How has the onboarding process gone?
- Has there been enough support to feel successful? What would you suggest from an improvement standpoint?
- How are you fitting in with the team?
- Do you believe you have the right tools to successfully do your job?
- Do you believe you have the right skills to do your job?
- How do you believe you are performing in your job?
- Is the salary/benefit expectation as described to you during the interview process?
- What is it that you really appreciate about working with/for [Company]?

- Any red flags that I should know about?
- Is there a question I didn't ask about something you wanted to share with me?

Manager One-on-One Guide

Used by managers and leaders. One-on-one meetings between an employee and their manager is considered a cornerstone for effective management to build trust, set the stage for open dialogue, and invite two-way feedback. Typically held every week and no less than one time each month for thirty minutes. To ensure effective and efficient meetings, ask your employees to be prepared with updates/topics. Sample questions could include:

- How are things going for you? (This could elicit a personal or work-related response.)
- What updates do you have to share since we last met/talked?
- What do you have on your plate?
- Do you need additional support or additional assignments?
- What other topics would you like to discuss?
- Where are you finding success?
- Where are you experiencing challenges?
- Feedback I'd like to provide to you is...
- What feedback do you have for me?
- How can I help you to be successful in your role?
- What can I do to support you?
- Are you experiencing any pain points in your role?
- What else would you like to share?

The 2x2 Feedback Model

This tool can be used between a manager and employee or two peers and is relatively simple to employ. The purpose of this tool is to create a foundation and natural exchange of open feedback. Sharing feedback creates both confidence and competence. After each exchange, it's important to express gratitude for the feedback.

- Manager says to employee, "Here are two things I think you are doing well and two things I think you can do better."
- Manager asks employee, "What are two things you think I am doing well and two things you think I can do better?"

Leadership Skip-Level Questions

Used by senior leaders to engage in conversation and exploration with "next level down" direct reports. Provides feedback and insights on how the senior leader's direct report is doing with managing their team.

- How are things going for you here at the company and with your job?
- What are a few of your greatest accomplishments?
- What is your manager doing well?
- What could your manager be doing better?
- What can you always count on your manager for?
- What can you never count on your manager for?
- How responsive is your manager to your daily/weekly requests (email, conversation, etc.)?
- How responsive is your manager in engaging with your personal and career development goals?
- When you describe your manager to friends and family, what do you say?
- What is the one thing your manager should never stop doing?
- What is one thing your manager should consider doing differently?
- Is there anything I didn't ask about that you would like to share?

Exit Interview

Exit interviews are used to provide insights for leaders about how the company is doing, to create or enhance current processes and procedures, and for employees to share their feedback when leaving an organization. In some cases, exit interviews can also prompt an employee to stay with an organization. Questions frequently used include:

- What circumstances prompted you to start looking for another job?
- Why are you leaving your job?
- What were the key factors in you deciding to take a new job?
- Salary? Benefits? Time off? Something else?
- Were you satisfied with your salary?
- How about the company's benefits package?
- Is there anything your new company offers that this company doesn't provide?
- What did you like best about your job?
- What did you like least about your job?
- Do you feel you had the tools, resources, and working conditions to be successful in your role? If not, how could it have been better?
- Was there anything especially challenging that you had to contend with?
- What would you change about your job?
- Did you receive enough training to do the job effectively?
- Did you receive enough support to do your job effectively?
- What did your manager do well?
- What could your manager do better?
- How do you feel about the feedback you received from your manager?
- What did you like best about working for the company?

- What did you like least about working for the company?
- Do you have any recommendations for the company for the future?
- Would you work for the company in the future?
- Would you recommend this company to prospective employees?
- Is there anything that I have not asked that you would like to share?
- What did you learn while working here?
- Do you have any questions or comments?

Acknowledgments

I have heartfelt gratitude for all the people in my life. Each of you in your own way has influenced how I view the world, how I create relationships, the way in which I cultivate business, how I coach, and how I lead.

Many of the ideas and stories contained in this book are a direct result of experiences throughout my career and life.

This book would not have been possible without my incredible writing dream team.

I am profoundly grateful to my writing coach, mentor, partner, and friend Mary Reynolds Thompson for providing clear guidance and direct feedback as these pages unfolded. She encouraged me to slow down when writing my stories. She advised me on how to restructure, revise and edit these pages to make the information more accessible to each reader. Her patience, intuition, deep listening and support allowed me to grow immensely during this process. Her experience and insights taught me a lot about writing a book. She also introduced me to the right team when it was time to bring this book to the public.

Martha Bullen has been the guiding hand behind the business of publishing this book. From the moment we met, she was an enthusiastic supporter and key resource for everything I needed to know to publish and market this book. She went above and beyond by assisting with minor editing and sharing her opinions on other details that would only improve the book for my readers.

Christy Day is the creator of the book cover art and interior design. Through her deep listening, she was able to incorporate both my business and whimsical self into the whole artistic design of this book.

David Aretha, provided the final and extremely helpful finishing editing touches. His keen eye and suggestions made this book so much better.

Elizabeth Teklits jumped into the mix with this writing dream team by providing clear operational and project management contributions. Her ability to create my book release roadmap was a piece of art and helped me clearly understand key deadlines. She kept me on track with this book while I was also managing my business. Elizabeth was the glue that kept everything together, communicating with each of the writing team members to ensure we were all on the same page (pun intended).

I would like to thank many of my colleagues and friends for listening to and supporting my dreams over the years. To my many bosses, thank you for sharing your leadership styles with me. I learned so much of what to do, what not to do, and what works for my unique style. To all the leaders I have had the honor to work with throughout my career: I have taken the best parts of my experiences with you and integrated them into who I want to be and how I want to show up as a leader.

Tom Rackerby, thank you for sharing the many sides of yourself. As a key leader and mentor in my life, you were the first leader that gave me a glimpse that we could operate as our whole selves at work. You taught me how to "keep things real."

Sheri Langford, over the past 30 plus years, we've spent a lot of long and late nights talking about our life paths and dreams. Thank you for how you've created balance for me. You've enthusiastically and realisitically supported my ideas. You have been my rock. I'm glad we've shared this journey together.

Sandy Naatz and Roberta Hayhurst, thank you for your continual words of encouragement.

Lisa Donile, in 2017 while we were backpacking in the Colorado mountains, you had a dream that you were selling my books. Without either of us knowing this, you planted a seed. Thanks for that!

Joyce Mirow, Karla Miller, and Barb Adams, thank you for your unwavering faith and feedback since our middle school years.

Kelley Ferguson, Meredith Mackert, Emily Inman, Teri Slenkovich, Tracey Ray, Tracy Crockett, Brooke Burgamy, Erika Young, Tad Deering, Don Becker, and other former colleagues, thank you for cheering me on when I started my consulting business.

Keith Crosson, Jay Fowler, Jim McComb, D. J. Smith, Mary Pray, J. D. Johnston, Duane Woods, and so many others in my music community—you've been invaluable feedback machines when it comes to playing music and sharing life together. Thank you!

To Stephanie Lovinger, Margo Boster, Susan Drumm, Dr. Beverly Kaye, Dr. Marcia Reynolds, Ph.D, Brad Harper, Michael Norton, Rose Snyder, Ashleigh Bechtel, Lynne Brown, Tracy Morrissey, Susan Williams, Lynne Williams, Kristy Thompson, Isabelle Tierney, Rachel Lutowsky, Eric Bailey, John Patterson, Lillie Richardson, Walt Richardson, Dan Fridena, Teri Spillan and so many others for encouraging and inspiring me to "show up" as the person I am.

To my mom, Frances Esther Neavill. Though our life together on earth lasted only fifteen years, you taught me the importance of integrity, tenacity, optimism, trust, a strong love for all humans, the importance of relationships, continual learning, to laugh often, to work hard, and to dance like no one is watching.

To my siblings, Mark Smith, Linda Garofalo, Kevin Smith, and Eric Rovlenchik. You remind me of the importance of our family love and strong bonds.

To my daughters, Elizabeth Teklits and Allyson Hibdon. As children you taught me how to never take myself too seriously, to be curious, and to play. As grown women, you continue to teach me that there are multiple ways to look at the world. I am in a constant state of wonder, joy, and pure love with you two.

To my husband, Dennis Hibdon. Thank you for your unconditional love and support, for listening to all my ideas and dreams, and for cooking nourishing and tasty food. You have taught me to be more spontaneous, to trust and to love more deeply. Your ideas, input, and feedback, and encouragement are invaluable. You make me a better human.

And finally, to Marc Willency, whose caring and courageous feedback changed my life.

References

Chapter 1: What Is Feedback?

1. Malcolm Timothy Gladwell. *Outliers: The Story of Success* (Little, Brown and Company, 2008), 35.
2. Charles Proteus Steinmetz. *Journal of the Franklin Institute*, July 1915.
3. Norbert Wiener. *The Human Use of Human Beings* (De Capo Press 1950), 58, 59.

Chapter 3: The Cost of Not Giving Feedback

4. Shari Harley. *How to Say Anything to Anyone* (Greenleaf Book Press, 2013). YouTube video https://www.youtube.com/watch?v=hYiHansSRrU, :23 - :46.
5. 2021 National Average Wage Index as reported by the Social Security Administration. https://www.ssa.gov/oact/cola/AWI.html

Chapter 4: How Energy Is A Form of Feedback

6. Dr. Albert Mehrabian. https://www.bl.uk/people/albert-mehrabian#:
7. The Principle of Least Effort was defined in 1894 by Italian philosopher Guillaume Ferrero in an article in the *Revue philosophique de la France et de l'étranger*.
8. Isabelle Tierney. Stress Reset™ https://thefeelgoodlife.com/the-stress-reset/
9. Energy through DK Learning. https://learning.dk.com/us/books/9781465451040/+dk+eyewitness+books+energy

Chapter 5: Creating the Optimal Environment for Feedback

10. Jim Dethmer, Diana Chapman, Kaley Warner Klemp. *The 15 Commitments of Conscious Leadership* (Dethmer, Chapman & Klemp 2015), 15.

11. Ben Casnocha. https://casnocha.com/about

Chapter 6: A Unique Way of Thinking About Feedback

12. First Hat. https://en.wikipedia.org/wiki/Hat

Chapter 7: Why Feedback Is Core to Leadership

13. SBI™. https://www.ccl.org/policies/trademarks/' https://www.ccl.org/articles/leading-effectively-articles/sbi-feed-back-model-a-quick-win-to-improve-talent-conversations-de-velopment/

14. Joseph Grenny, Kerry Patterson, Ron McMillan, Al Switzler, Emily Gregory. *Crucial Conversations When the Stakes are High*—Third Edition (McGraw Hill, 2022).

15. Zippia. https://www.zippia.com/advice/employee-feed-back-statistics/

16. Oprah Winfrey & Jeff Weiner, CEO of LinkedIn. https://www.youtube.com/watch?v=S-QNwKiu5xU

Chapter 8: Things That Get in the Way of Giving Feedback

17. 2022 Gallup Study. https://www.gallup.com/work-place/349484/state-of-the-global-workplace.aspx

18. Rick Hanson, Ph.D. *Hardwiring Happiness* (Harmony Books, NY, 2013).

19. Benedictine University. Why is Everyone Talking about Feed-back? (2019). https://cvdl.ben.edu/blog/why-is-everyone-talking-about-feedback/

20. Brené Brown, Ph.D. MsW. *Dare to Lead* (Random House, 2018).

Chapter 9: Ghosting: A Contemporary Twist on Feedback (Or What's Happened to Completion)

21. Zippia. https://www.zippia.com/answers/how-many-people-quit-their-jobs-in-2021/
22. Visier. https://www.visier.com/blog/survey-recruitment-ghosting/
23. Quora. https://www.quora.com/topic/Ghosting
24. Loren Soeiro, Ph.D. *7 Essential Psychological Truths About Ghosting.* https://www.psychologytoday.com/us/blog/i-hear-you/201902/7-essential-psychological-truths-about-ghosting
25. Ghosting added to the dictionary: 2017. https://www.merriam-webster.com/words-at-play/ghosting-words-were-watching#

Chapter 10: Being on the Receiving End of Feedback

26. Carol Dweck, Ph.D. *Mindset: The New Psychology of Success* (Ballentine Books, NY, 2006).

About the Author

Joan (Joni) Hibdon, CPCC, PCC

Cultivating cultures where people thrive is what Joan is passionate about. She has gained the reputation of being a trusted advisor, coach, and valuable business partner. Through executive coaching, Joan helps leaders discover the best version of themselves, allowing them to exceed their potential and feel fulfilled in their lives. The impact of executives and leaders who experience personal transformation creates high-performing cultures. Joan's experience in this area has proven that with the right leaders, teams and individuals, extraordinary performance results can be achieved. Her ability to listen to others and share critical insights is essential for human and business results.

Joan has spent her career leading various human resource functions, working across diverse global industries including financial, cable, food services, software, and telecommunications. In addition to having expertise in executive coaching and leadership development, Joan knows how to align business strategy with human performance, create organizational and team effectiveness, and lead change management efforts. Joan believes that making an investment in people has a direct correlation to being a competitive differentiator for companies in their industry marketplace.

Companies Joan has worked for include Luman (formerly CenturyLink), Level 3 Communications, tw telecom, Webroot Software, JD Edwards, PeopleSoft (now Oracle), Reiss Media, and Time Warner Cable. Joan has provided coaching solutions for organizations in the medical, professional services, academic, oil & gas, telecommunications, insurance, digital marketing, software, and food service industries.

Joan is a Denver, Colorado native and currently lives in Glendale, Arizona with her husband, Dennis, and their goldendoodle, Miliani. Joan graduated from the University of Phoenix with a bachelor's degree in business management. She holds several certifications in Leadership Coaching and Team Effectiveness including but not limited to The Leadership Circle Profile, iEQ9 (Enneagram), iEQ-2.0, DiSC, and The Myers Briggs Type Indicator (MBTi). In her spare time, Joan loves hanging out with her two daughters, entertaining friends, cycling, backpacking, sailing, and performing in various music venues.

To learn more or contact Joan, please visit www.jdhinsights.com.

Manufactured by Amazon.ca
Bolton, ON

39082887R10133